A Physical Walk with God

A Physical Walk with God…

…to the cross roads of greater health.

Mark Joseph Geiger

Edited and Published by Mark Geiger, Healthy
Images in Irving, TX

Note for Librarians: A cataloguing record for this book is available from Library and Archives
Canada at www.collectionscanada.ca/amicus/index-e.html
ISBN 1-4120-8013-4

*Printed in Victoria, BC, Canada. Printed on paper with minimum 30% recycled fibre. Trafford's print shop
runs on "green energy" from solar, wind and other environmentally-friendly power sources.*

Offices in Canada, USA, Ireland and UK
This book was published *on-demand* in cooperation with Trafford Publishing. On-demand
publishing is a unique process and service of making a book available for retail sale to the
public taking advantage of on-demand manufacturing and Internet marketing. On-demand
publishing includes promotions, retail sales, manufacturing, order fulfilment, accounting and
collecting royalties on behalf of the author.

Book sales for North America and international:
Trafford Publishing, 6E–2333 Government St.,
Victoria, BC v8t 4p4 CANADA
phone 250 383 6864 (toll-free 1 888 232 4444)
fax 250 383 6804; email to orders@trafford.com
Book sales in Europe:
Trafford Publishing (uk) Limited, 9 Park End Street, 2nd Floor
Oxford, UK oxi 1hh UNITED KINGDOM
phone 44 (0)1865 722 113 (local rate 0845 230 9601)
facsimile 44 (0)1865 722 868; info.uk@trafford.com
Order online at:
trafford.com/05-3011

10 9 8 7 6 5 4 3 2 1

Acknowledgments

To my wife Lisa, thanks for your patience. Not just for the time it took for me to write this book, but for me to live what lay within these pages. I am excited about the life of ministry that God has purposed for us and am thankful because next to His son, you are His greatest gift to me.

Thank you to Tony and Nelly. Tony, you told me I needed to develop a faith based exercise program long before I could ever even hear the voice of God for myself. You truly are a prophet. Thanks for your friendship and your investment in my life.

Thanks to Dennis, my loving Hebrew friend who is a great man of Faith, your blind generosity paved the way and helped lay the foundation for the experiences in this book. Many people's lives have been introduced into the Kingdom of God because you shared your wealth. Your true riches are in heaven.

To Marty and Bobby, thank you for my first bible and for plugging me into IBC. Blessings to your family.

To Scotty and Matt, thanks for your unconditional friendships. Scotty I am proud of you. Matt, I am proud of you too and my prayer is that someday you will understand and experience the truths in this book.

Thank you to my family, especially my parents, for your love, patience and prayers.

Thank you to the Cottonwood bunnies for your friendship and support so many years ago.

Thank you to Covenant Church for my covering and to Pastor G for your inspiration and encouragement.

Foreword by
Dr. E. Andrew McQuitty

As a pastor and an athlete over the years, I've always appreciated Paul's words to young Timothy:

"Have nothing to do with godless myths and old wives' tales; rather, train yourself to be godly. For physical training **is** *of some value, but godliness has value for all things, holding promise for both the present life and the life to come."*

1 Timothy 4:7-8

Paul is keen to promote godliness, and every dedicated follower of Jesus resonates with that challenge. But sometimes in that verse we miss Paul's promotion of *physical training* as well. Sure, Paul indicates that on God's priority scale for our lives, physical fitness falls below godliness. But it does receive an honorable mention! That's because God knows that all the godliness in the world needs a body for expression. We are soul-body unities as human beings, and therefore taking care of our physical bodies is as spiritual a discipline as there is. The problem is that believers have rarely been instructed in the why and the how: from a spiritual standpoint, why is it important to keep fit, and how do we do it?

I am just delighted to see that my friend Mark Geiger has plugged that gap for the church with his excellent book <u>A</u>

<u>Physical Walk with God</u>. This unique guide takes us through a devotional and physical workout that ministers to the soul and strengthens the body at the same time. From my times of sweating, praying, lifting weights and discussing the things of God in Mark's personal training studios, I can vouch for the effectiveness of his approach from personal experience. Mark not only knows kinesiology, He knows God. And that's a dynamic combination!

Table of Contents

Acknowledgements   5

Foreword by Dr. E. Andrew McQuitty   6

Preface   11

1. The Cross Roads   17

    Nutrition
    Cardiovascular
    Resistance Training
    Flexibility

2. The New (*and Final*) Covenant   53

3. Patience   71

4. Discipleship   89

5. Support   111

6. Accountability   129

7. Suffering   147

8. Attitude   165

9. The Truth   193

10. Self Image   215

11. The Desert/Plateau &
    Your Insatiable Hunger   237

12. The Ultimate Bodybuilders   259

Finding a Trainer Checklist   289

Preface

This is not your typical health and fitness book that promises you'll lose weight and get in great shape if you just follow the latest and greatest workout program. The truth is that great physical health is achievable by any number of the programs that are already available on the market today. As much as the health and fitness industry would like you to believe that they are constantly coming out with new and innovative ways of getting in shape, the reality is that the science and exercise principles are always the same. The science of exercise has not changed since God first created it. It's always the same basic concept with a slightly different look, a different name or a better marketing spin. If people would just follow the basic science of exercise they would be successful whether they were using machines or free weights; whether they were walking on the treadmill or climbing the Stairmaster. It all works. Even some of those annoying infomercial products work.

No, the challenge lies in our heads and in our hearts. The real challenge lies in what we believe about ourselves, what we believe about God, and what we think God and other people believe about us. If we can get to the truth of these cores issues then we can begin to truly understand that being healthy is not solely dependent on what size clothing we wear or how we look in a mirror or bathing suit. Instead, if we can get to the truth, we will find that we were in fact created in the healthiest image of God.

With that in mind, *A Physical Walk with God* is designed to take you through a twelve week study of the core issues that affect individual and family health dynamics. Issues such as covenant commitments, forgiveness, patience, endurance, discipleship, and suffering are just to name a few. While this twelve week study is designed for you to exercise as you read through each week's material, it is not an in depth scientific look at exercise and nutrition. It does not offer a complicated or highly complex exercise routine or diet to follow. Instead it offers a simple outline of easy to understand guidelines that anyone can follow. It also focuses profoundly on spiritual truth, scriptural principles, and how to overcome harmful mind-sets that keep us from doing the things we know we should be doing and all the things we know God wants us to be doing.

Furthermore, this book was written after a decade of personal and professional experiences in dealing with both healthy and un-healthy individuals. It was also written after determining that the solutions to our health problems cannot be solved simply by buying gym memberships, and diet or exercise products. If that was the solution, our obesity rate, health problems and health insurance costs would not all still be skyrocketing. No, the solution to our health problems are found in the on-going personal instruction, the on-going personal teaching... the on-going **personal training** of individuals and small groups. It is a fact that the people who seek personal training are far more likely to achieve results, and faster, than those who attempt to diet and exercise on their own.

You went to school and were taught your trade. Chances are, someone showed you how to perform and do the things you do barring a few exceptions. My point is that I don't think the majority of people can effectively read this book or any other book and achieve the optimal results in the shortest period of time. I would be lying to sell more books if I touted this.

So instead of simply publishing a book and leaving you to fend for yourself like many of the products on the market today; the Healthy Images Preventative Health Care Organization was founded to be a back bone of support to this book and program.

Healthy Images vision and mission is to build the body of Christ one soul at a time by helping churches establish fitness rooms on their campuses. And not only that, but Healthy

Images also provides a personal training staff and or the necessary education to selected staff members of the churches who join our organizations.

If you are moved to transform your health or help transform the health of those around you then please, go to our website and contact us at www.healthyimages.org

Father, bless your children who are reading this book right now. Overwhelm them with your Holy Spirit; give them understanding, hope, peace, and courage to persevere as they invite you to teach them about the physical nature you've designed in and for them.

Instructions on how to use this book

Read the pre-workout information in the back of the book, page 280, before beginning any of the physical exercises.

Read one chapter per week while performing the coinciding and suggested spiritual and physical exercises at the end of each chapter. Be sure to rely on your personal trainer, or small group members to stick with the program.

The program lasts twelve weeks and with the help of the Holy Spirit, it will totally transform every aspect of your life.

Chapter One

The Cross Roads

*"Stand at the **crossroads** and look; ask for the ancient paths, ask where the good way is, and walk in it, and you will find rest for your souls.*

Jeremiah 6:16

So you have come to that point in your journey where you have to make the decision. Your whole Christian life you have come to the cross and then left for a while, come to the cross, and then left for a while in an endless cycle. When I say "left" I am not speaking in absolute terms. I am not talking about complete abandonment of God or your Faith. No what I am talking about is turning away from principles you've already learned, principles God has already painstakingly taught you.

As I watch people in their quest for better physical health I have found that there is often a parallel between their physical walk with God and their spiritual walk with Him. In both walks their good habits often lack commitment and consistency. In the physical I have watched people learn the four principles of health, work extremely hard at implementing them into their daily lives, and achieve success whether it was with weight loss or some other goal. Unfortunately not all of these people went the distance. Not all of them were able to maintain their accomplishments and they eventually digressed in their habits and health again.

I have seen the same thing in the spiritual. In fact I have experienced the same thing. There were times when I had specific sins in my life and I took them to the cross. I asked God to remove them and to help me repent from them only to once again succumb to them months or even years later. Why is it that we do this? Why is it that we start a healthy lifestyle or fitness program and then stop? Why is it that we stop sins and then start them again? Paul spoke of this "phenomenon" when he said, *"For what I do is not the good I want to do; no, the evil I do not want to do--this I keep on doing."* (Romans 7:19)

Every time I read that passage I can almost hear the frustration in his voice. I would propose that in part, and aside from our immaturity, one reason for this is our lack of understanding of what a covenant is. In the following chapter we will look at what a covenant is and why it is so important to be in Covenant with God when it comes to your health. With a deeper understanding of what a covenant with God means, it is likely we won't have to keep coming back to the cross with the same sins and the same unhealthy habits. Instead we can stay on the cross roads. But for this first chapter our focus will be on the **basic** eating and exercise principles that are going to help you become healthier.

Now, as you read through these next four sections, be sure you understand there is a pattern. Each section will begin with the benefits (blessings) you'll receive when following the principles, and then it will go on to show you that there truly is a connection between the physical and the spiritual, that in fact they mirror each other. We must remember that God is physical in nature and not just spiritual and that there are in fact instructions (scripture) that indicate how we should act accordingly.

As illustrated by the diagram on the next page, there are four health and fitness components that need to be addressed in order to achieve and maintain good health, no more, no less. It is this simple. If you will address each one of these components, introducing them into your life, all at the same time, you will not only achieve results but you will do it quicker than most people who only address one at a time here and there.

The Cross Roads

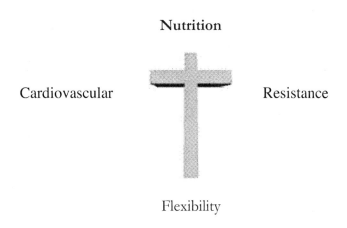

Nutrition

Cardiovascular   Resistance

Flexibility

Nutrition

Let's start with the most important component first. Nutrition is approximately 80% of a person's success. Having a healthy diet is one of the most important ways you can maintain an active lifestyle and protect against health problems. Maintaining and active lifestyle is especially important for Christians if we are going to serve others. Eating well also increases energy, improves the way the body functions, strengthens your immune system and prevents weight problems.

Even more specifically, a healthy diet helps you:

- **Meet your nutritional needs** - A varied, balanced diet provides the nutrients you need to avoid nutritional deficiencies. Non-nutrients, such as fiber, also are a part of your nutritional needs.
- **Prevent and treat certain diseases** - Your diet can prevent the risk of developing certain diseases such as cancer and heart disease. It is also helpful in treating

diabetes and high blood pressure. Following a special diet can reduce symptoms and may help you better manage a disease or reduce your need for costly prescription drugs.

- **Enjoy life** - Food is an important part of social and cultural events. Not only does it provide nutrition, but it can facilitate connections between people.
- **Feel energetic and manage your weight** - A healthy diet will also make you feel better, give you more energy, and help you fight physical and emotional stress.

A person can work on the other three components of the crossroads and achieve some results but neglecting the crucial component of nutrition usually undermines the rest of their efforts. The following is a simple easy to understand *overview* of basic nutritional principles that will help you in your physical walk with God. As I said in the preface, there are plenty of complex and in-depth studies on the matter but the main and ladder focus of this book is on the spiritual issues that will help us <u>follow</u> these principles.

At Healthy Images we believe that God made eating so simple that even small children could understand how to do it correctly. We also believe our food is color coded and that different foods are to be eaten in balance but at specific times of the day. The six steps on the following pages correlate to the color coded diagram and will help you understand which foods metabolize the fastest and what time of day you should eat them to ensure that you give your body ample time to digest them before completing your daily activities. The steps to understanding this diagram are outlined, just follow the colors keeping in mind the idea of the traffic light and what the different colors tells us to do!

Red equals stop.

Yellow equals proceed with caution.

Green equals go!

Follow the Signals!

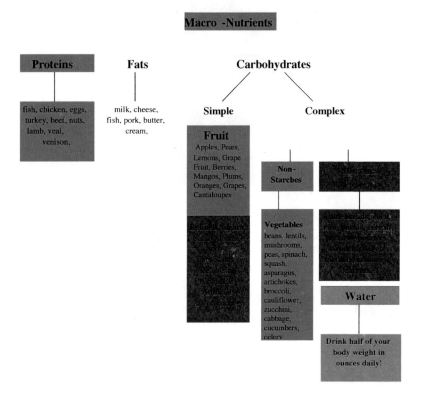

Macro -Nutrients

Proteins — fish, chicken, eggs, turkey, beef, nuts, lamb, veal, venison,

Fats — milk, cheese, fish, pork, butter, cream,

Carbohydrates

Simple

Fruit
Apples, Pears, Lemons, Grape Fruit, Berries, Mangos, Plums, Oranges, Grapes, Cantaloupes

Complex

Non-Starches

Vegetables
beans. lentils, mushrooms, peas, spinach, squash, asparagus, artichokes, broccoli, cauliflower, zucchini, cabbage, cucumbers, celery

Water

Drink half of your body weight in ounces daily!

Step 1   Eat the foods in green at every meal (including breakfast). **But** only eat fruits early in the day.

Step 2   Use caution when eating foods in the yellow. Eat less than 30 grams of fat per day. It is easy to count fat grams. Just look at the label and keep a running mental log. If you dine out and there is no label, it is likely that you are going to get at least 10 grams of fat in a meal unless you are eating at a healthy restaurant.

Step 3   Eat foods in red early in the day also. For weight loss purposes do not eat more than three starches per day.

Step 4   Do not eat foods in red after 3 pm. Your body is less likely to metabolize them before the end of the day meaning they could get stored as reserve energy or excess body fat while you sleep.

Step 5   Refined and Artificial Sugars such as sweet and low, aspartame, saccharin, and stevia cause your hormones to fluctuate and can in turn cause fatigue and excess body fat storage. **Therefore it is best to totally avoid them, especially the diet sodas.**

Step 6   Drink at least half of your body weight in ounces of water each day.

Ex: If you weigh 200 pounds you need to drink 100 ounces of water per day.

That may sound like a lot of water but it is necessary to help transport your food through your body. Also, by drinking that much water it will help fill you up making less room for food.

Following these six simple colored coded steps alone will change your life. You will feel great, lose weight, and have more energy. Also, please know, these steps are in fact biblical. For example, *Moses also said, "You will know that it was the Lord when he gives you meat to eat in the evening and all the bread you want in the morning, because he has heard your grumbling against him."* (Exodus 16:8) That scripture supports and is in agreement with steps 1, 3, and 4!

Another example is after Jesus died and rose again he appeared three times. The third time He appeared was to have breakfast with Simon Peter, Thomas, and two other apostles. The apostles were out fishing in the Sea of Tiberius and had not caught anything all night. Jesus showed up early in the morning, calling out to them to cast there nets on the right side of the boat where they would find the fish. (It was breakfast time… and Jesus wanted His lean protein.) Peter immediately recognized Jesus and headed for the shore. The other disciples towed the net in behind the boat because it was too full of fish to lift out of the water. Jesus specifically said to them, *"Come and have breakfast"…Jesus came, took the bread and gave it to them, and did the same with the fish.* (John 21:12-13)

The disciples then ate breakfast with Jesus, who had supplied the bread to go with their fish. Jesus knew the bread, or as we call it today, the starchy carbohydrate, was important for His disciples to eat early in the day because it would give them lasting energy throughout the day. He also knew that the fish would balance out the meal, their hormones, and serve as a building block for there bodies. The bible doesn't mention what they had to drink with their breakfast but I doubt it was a double capo chino from Starbucks. If I had to guess I would say they drank water. I'll bet they blessed their food that morning too. This account of scripture also supports and is in agreement with steps 1 and 3.

I can't stress enough how very important it is to pay close attention to the foods in red. This category is primarily what trips people up, both the simple sugars and the complex. It is important to understand not all starches and other carbohydrates are made the same. Though breads, bagels, pastas, crackers and tortillas are low fat foods, they are usually processed and have a much higher glycemic index; meaning they take longer for your body to metabolize. Much of their nutritional values, the important vitamins and minerals, are unfortunately removed during the processing which actually makes them empty calories. One way to avoid these is by not purchasing products that are labeled "enriched". Instead, purchase your products from a whole foods source.

Though some of the foods in red can be eaten in moderation, naturally occurring complex carbohydrates are best for leaning down. They include: brown, wild and long grain rice, small potatoes, yams, kidney beans, black beans, pinto beans, and couscous.

Before going on you really need to ask yourself if you are a carbohydrate junkie. Do you love simple sugars...diet sodas, candy, and juice. Or, are you a complex carbohydrate junkie who loves pasta, potatoes and bread. If you are and you want to lose weight then you need to **pray** about this, **act** according to the six steps above, and then **wait** patiently!

People are always praying about things like money, jobs, marriages, and even sometimes about their health and weight loss. But when they don't see the immediate and expected results of their prayers they question God's existence. And even if they still believe He exists, then they question whether or not He loves them or cares about their prayers. I propose that one of the reasons why our prayers are not always answered in our time frame is because we are not feeding on the right kind of bread...the word of God. Instead, we are feeding and relying entirely on our own worldly efforts. Jesus tells us very clearly ...*The Scriptures say, 'People need more than bread for their life; they must feed on every word of God."* (Matthew 4:4)

God does speak to us. He does answers our prayers, and one of the ways He does it is by leading us to specific passages in the bible. He "**feeds**" us the information we are looking for. He "**feeds**" us the answers to our prayers by what He says in His word. The question is...are we eating it? Are we consuming it? Is it becoming a building block within our bodies and our lives? You see it is not enough to read or "know" the word of God. God can only answer your prayers and help you achieve the desires of your heart if you are willing to, by Faith, consume (eat) what it is you have read. It has to become a part of your life, your speech, and your daily actions. You cannot pray to God like a Jeanie in a lamp expecting effortless results. Nor can you use Him like the Internet to simply seek information. Your actions have to indicate to Him and those around you that you believe what you read.

Friends, I would propose that if you have an unquenchable appetite for anything...food, money, work, sex, or drugs, then perhaps you've never eaten of the bread of life. Once you have eaten the type of bread I am talking about you'll never be the same. You will be hungry but it will not be for anything in this world.

Follow the cross! It will help you lose weight and become healthier!

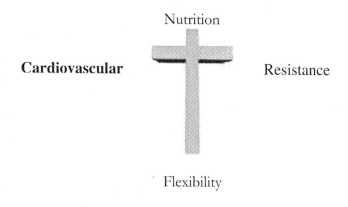

Nutrition

Cardiovascular Resistance

Flexibility

Cardiovascular

The second component on the cross road to health that needs to be addressed is cardiovascular exercise. Also called aerobic exercise, cardio is any type of exercise that increases your breathing and heart rate, thus improving the condition of your heart and lungs. Besides providing these and other numerous health benefits (blessings), cardiovascular exercise also burns off excess calories. Cardiovascular exercise encompasses many types of exercise including, but not limited to the activities on the next page.

Now if the physical benefits (blessings) aren't enough to make you get off the couch and tie your shoes right now then what about the fact that God was and still is BIG on the idea of us walking. All through out both the Hebrew Testament and the New Testament we find scripture that illustrates this truth. Knowing that God is both a physical God and a spiritual God we have to look at the word "walk" from both perspectives. It is obvious that the physical perspective refers to the cardio we are speaking of above. However, from a spiritual perspective, the word walk refers to a person's level of obedience to the instructions of God.

• Aerobic dance classes	• Running
• Basketball	• Skiing (or snowboarding)
• Chasing your dog or kids	• Soccer
• Cycling	• Spinning
• Dancing	• Stair climbing
• Field Hockey	• Swimming
• Golf (without a cart)	• Tennis
• Hiking	• Vigorous yoga (such as Bikram)
• Kick boxing	• Walking
• Rope skipping	• Water aerobics
• Rowing	

The best scripture for proving that God wants us to walk both physically and spiritually is, *"Walk in the way that the Lord your God has commanded you, so that you may live and prosper and prolong your days in the land that you will posses."* (Deuteronomy 5:33)

Here we see that God refers to the physical life span by using the phrase "prolong your days", and also that if we follow His commands, (walk in his ways) we will *prosper*, which is a spiritual principle and promise.

Wait a minute…you mean there is a relationship between a persons **walk** in obedience to God's commandments and prosperity? Yes, absolutely! There are accounts all over the Hebrew Testament where obedience led to prosperity and there lack of led to poverty and death. Judah had a total of 20 kings after Solomon's reign. Only eight of them gave Godly moral and spiritual leadership. And as the king went, so went the nation. *But remember the Lord your God, for it is he who gives you the* *ability to produce wealth, and so confirms his covenant, which he swore to your forefathers, as it is today.* **(Deuteronomy 8:18)**

Another excellent passage that absolutely convicted me of both this physical and spiritual truth was when the prophet Jeremiah said, *This is what the Lord says: "Stand at the* **crossroads** *and look; ask for the ancient paths, ask where the good way is, and walk in it, and you will find rest for your souls.* (Jeremiah 6:16) The *ancient paths* were and are the tried and true ways of Judah's godly ancestors. And *you will find rest for your soul"* was again promised and quoted by Jesus. (Mt 11:29) Friends you and I are at the cross roads. We have to make a decision. Until we commit to a consistent spiritual and physical walk with the Lord we will not find rest.

Many people say they do not exercise in general because of time constraints or financial reasons. As you can see many of the things on the previous list do not cost anything and can be done without the expenses associated with joining a health club. Regarding the issue of time, I have always encouraged my clients that if their time is limited, to combine their prayer time with their cardiovascular exercise time. Some of the greatest conversations and some of the greatest revelations I have ever had have occurred on my *physical walks* with God. Too many of us get caught up in the idea that prayer is for a quiet time and in an isolated place but we must remember that Paul taught us to pray about all things without ceasing. (Ephesians 6:18)

In closing out this section on cardio, one fairly common question that I get asked a lot is *"which exercise is best to do and yields the greatest results?"* My response to that is; don't get caught up too much in the scientific business but instead, just get down to business. Do the one that appeals to you the most, fits into your schedule the best, and is most appropriate to your current level of fitness. If you do not know your current level of fitness or where to start, I would again recommend getting guidance from a qualified personal trainer. Besides that, you should always consult a physician prior to starting any health and fitness program.

At the end of each chapter you will find suggestions for cardiovascular exercise and a place to record your activities.

Follow the cross! It will help you lose weight and become healthier!

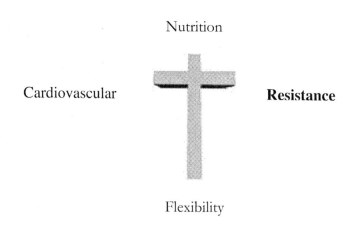

Nutrition

Cardiovascular   **Resistance**

Flexibility

Resistance

The third component on the cross road to health is resistance training. As if you don't already have enough resistance in your daily life, now you have healthcare professionals telling you to add more. Resistance or weight training involves using different muscle groups to lift weights. This is not limited to lifting huge barbells, but also includes such simple things as raising the legs with ankle weights attached. In recent years the fitness industry has developed simple ways to exercise in the home with small affordable tools such as bands, balls and other various home gym equipment. In the week one exercises you will find some suggestions for home exercise equipment.

Resistance training has benefits (blessings) that differ from cardiovascular training and therefore compliments it well. Some of those benefits include:

1. Improved neural motor skills, coordination, balance and strength
2. Improved bone density
3. A stronger heart muscle
4. Improved muscular endurance (Energy!)

5. Improved resting metabolic rate (Enhanced calorie and fat burning at rest!)
6. Stronger immunity to illness and disease

Another great benefit to resistance training is whereas cardiovascular exercise melts away superficial fat around the waist, resistance training has been found to dissolve the innermost fat around internal organs. So a combined effort of both cardio and resistance training is beneficial in that they decrease the chance for obesity, osteoporosis, diabetes, cardiovascular disease and in older people the number of accidental falls that lead to temporary or permanent immobility and inactivity.

If you've never attempted any type of resistance exercise it is never to late to start. I had the chance and was actually blessed by the opportunity to train a 75 year old man named Asa who had had a heart attack and stroke both. Prior to his personal training he had smoked for over 50 years and had never done any kind of physical activity. After the stroke he had lost the use of his left arm. Within just a few weeks of limited resistance training and P.N.F. stretching he was able to begin using it again. After several months he had almost completely regained normal functioning of it. Not only that but he also received many of the benefits listed above. All things considered, if Asa could begin a resistance training program than anybody should be able to.

Regarding the spiritual aspect of resistance training, there is again a parallel. The spiritual principle reflects the physical. Just like with weight training, when you apply a force to your muscles they tear. You become tired and you have to feed them food to build them back up. The end result of this process is your muscles get bigger, harder, and stronger. The same is true with your soul. The devil is applying forces of evil to your life and all around it because he wants to rob kill and destroy. (John 10:10)

All of us need to resist him (temptation and sin). During this process of resistance, even with our best efforts, we sometimes get torn down both spiritually and emotionally. This resistance takes its toll on us and just as our physical muscles need food to heal, so do our hearts and minds. What heals us specifically is the word of God. You will find that "eating" the word of God is a frequent teaching in this book and in your physical walk with God.

Jesus told us...*I am the living bread that came down from heaven. If anyone eats of this bread, he will live forever. This bread is my flesh...* (John 6:51). Looking back at John 1:1 and remembering that God was both the flesh and the Word helps us make sense of this passage and this spiritual principle. In essence what he was telling us was to feed on his word. The biggest part of our spiritual resistance training is simply reading and doing the word of God. Both Peter and James knew the value of this and therefore specifically spoke of resistance training. "*Be self-controlled and alert. Your enemy the devil prowls like a roaring lion looking for someone to devour.* **Resist** *him, standing firm in the faith, because you know that your brothers throughout the world are undergoing the same kind of sufferings.* (1 Peter 5:8-9)

Also, James advises, "*Submit yourselves, then, to God.* **Resist** *the devil, and he will flee from you. Come near to God and he will come near to you.* (James 4:7-8)

From both of these scriptures we can see that spiritual resistance training is as simple as staying alert, submitting to God, and staying close to Him all of which can be done by studying His Word. And if that is not motivating enough, then know that both physical resistance training and spiritual resistance training are again mandates (instructions) from God. Timothy writes... "*train yourself to be Godly. For physical training is of some value, but godliness has value for all things, holding promise for both the present life and the life to come.*" (1 Timothy 4:7-8)

So what are you waiting for? Get started today! At the end of each chapter, along with weekly suggestions for your cardiovascular exercise, you will also find suggestions for resistance training. In addition to the suggestions, on the CD-Rom that came with this book you will be able to watch video demonstrations of how to perform the suggested exercises properly.

Follow the cross. It will help you lose weight and become healthier!

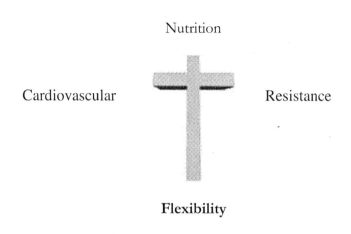

Nutrition

Cardiovascular   Resistance

Flexibility

Flexibility

Flexibility is the final component. Flexibility is a joint's ability to move through a full range of motion. Flexibility training (stretching) helps balance muscle groups that might be overused during exercise or physical activity or as a result of bad posture. There are many benefits that result from a good stretching program. The benefits (blessings) include:

1. Reduced Risk of Low Back Pain
2. Enhanced Enjoyment of Physical Activities
3. Reduced Muscle Soreness and Improved Posture
4. Improved Physical Performance and Decreased Risk of Injury
5. Increased Blood and Nutrients to Tissues
6. Improved Muscle Coordination

Flexibility is often the most overlooked component of the cross roads. I know I didn't place enough value on it early in my life.

When I was 21 years old and invincible I would consistently do the first three components but always ignored stretching. It soon caught up with me. The stronger I got from lifting weights the tighter my muscles got until one day I discovered the hard way that stretching cannot be overlooked. I was in the gym one afternoon in college and was doing some dead lifts when all of the sudden I heard and felt a debilitating "pop". After being laid up for several weeks, to the point I had to crawl whenever I was out of bed you can bet I did some serious soul searching. After months of seeing numerous doctors, chiropractors, specialists, having MRI's, and taking pain medication, the only thing that made my pain go away was an aggressive stretching routine.

Our spiritual lives are often a lot like my injury. We don't like to and won't do something until we absolutely or tragically have to. That is why God often times has to "encourage" us to stretch, our faith that is. We know that we are supposed to be stretched by our faith; that we are to live by faith and not by sight (2 Corinthians 5:7) but many of us do not. Stretching is a biblical command, and when we do it, it benefits us both physically and spiritually. The bible actually says we are "commended" for it. Read the following passage from Hebrews and maybe you will see what I mean.

Now faith is being sure of what we hope for and certain of what we do not see. This is what the ancients were commended for. **By faith** *we understand that the universe was formed at God's command, so that what is seen was not made out of what was visible.* **By faith Abel** *offered God a better sacrifice than Cain did.* **By faith he was commended** *as a righteous man, when God spoke well of his offerings. And* **by faith** *he still speaks, even though he is dead.* **By faith Enoch** *was taken from this life, so that he did not experience death; he could not be found, because God had taken him away. For before he was taken,* **he was commended** *as one who pleased God. And without faith it is impossible to please God, because anyone who comes to him must believe that he exists and that he rewards those who earnestly seek him.* **By faith Noah,** *when warned about things not yet seen, in holy fear built an ark to save his family. By his faith he condemned the world and became heir of the* *righteousness that comes by faith.* **By faith Abraham,** *when called to go to a place he would later receive as his inheritance, obeyed and went, even though he did not know where he was going.* **By faith** *he made his home in the Promised Land like a stranger in a foreign country; he lived in tents, as did Isaac and Jacob, who were heirs with him of the same promise. For he was looking forward to the city with foundations, whose architect and builder is God.* **By faith Abraham,** *even though he was past age--and Sarah herself was barren--was enabled to become a father because he considered him faithful who had made the promise. And so from this one man, and he as good as dead, came descendants as numerous as the stars in the sky and as countless as the sand on the seashore. All these people were still living* **by faith** *when they died.* (Hebrews 11:1-13)

Was it not a stretch for all of those people to believe and do all of the things God promised and told them to do? These were the heroes, the hall of famers when it came to stretching. What about you? Are you stretching both physically and spiritually? Did God tell you to marry that girl and you haven't done it yet? Did He tell you to leave that company and start your own but you still have yet to do it? Did He tell you to get off the couch and start that fitness program in your church but you're unsure where to begin? I highly recommend you voluntarily stretch yourself gently because sometimes when God has to do it is not always gentle.

Not convinced yet? Let me share another personal story about a client of mine. Jeff was a good man, very successful, hard working, gentle, and a family man. But during his young adult years he neglected all of the components of the cross roads only to wake up one morning at the age of 45 discovering that he had serious health issues that needed to be addressed. After signing up and making a commitment to personally train with me he lost 35 pounds, became stronger, had more energy, and overall had a better quality of life. Unfortunately he really needed to lose another 25 pounds. A year and a half went by while he was stuck at the same weight and it began to weigh on his emotions. He was working really hard and eating somewhat right but he just couldn't take it to the next level. The next level included a higher intensity cardio routine and lifting heavier weight. Jeff could not do this though because whenever we tried to increase the intensity it would always hurt his joints. The bottom line is Jeff lacked *flexibility*. He would never let me stretch him out because it hurt too much. Finally, after a couple of months of regular and consistent stretching, Jeff was able to make that break through and get to where he needed to be. *The question remains for you. Are you going to get to where you need to be both physically and spiritually by stretching?*

God wants us to mature in our relationship with Him and each other. The only way for us to do that is to stretch beyond our normal comfort level. Since everyone is in their own personal place with God that means we all need to be stretched differently. Some of us need to stretch by just accepting Jesus Christ as the Son of God and as our personal savior. Some of us who have already done that need to stretch by joining a church. Some of us who are already members of a church need to start helping support all the costs that the church incurs for helping us grow spiritually. Some of us who are already tithing need to be stretched by praying and reading the bible daily...not just on Sundays. You see, all of us can be stretched in some new way.

You maybe asking yourself; why do I need to stretch? Because that is what Christ did! He stretched His arms from east to west for you on the cross. Never will God ask you to make that kind of stretch, so, in comparison, all others stretches are easy.

In closing out this section on the component of flexibility, I firmly believe, because it is true, that God stretches our Faith...our ability to believe in the unseen. God designed our muscles to improve in function when we stretch them out; why would He not design our Faith the same way? We may choose not to stretch our muscles, but God stretches our Faith whether we like it or not. He does this because He wants us to know He is there and that He is providing for our needs beyond our own natural abilities.

40

At the end of the chapter, along with suggestions for your cardiovascular exercise, and resistance training you will find questions and spiritual stretching exercises. You will also find video demonstrations of some basic stretches on the CD-Rom.

Follow the cross. It will help you lose weight and become healthier!

That concludes our overview of the "scientific" part of this physical walk with God. These four principles, **nutrition, cardio, resistance,** and **flexibility** in and of themselves are not complicated or difficult. But what is complicated is our world and lives, our emotions and feelings. The rest of this book is now going to focus on what is going on inside of each of us and what is going on around each of us. While it only took me a few years in college to learn about exercise and nutrition, it has taken nearly a decade of trials, experiences, suffering, conquering, and prayers to be able to share what is in the rest of this book.

From this point on you should only read one chapter per week and then, throughout the rest of the week, meditate on the content. After reading each chapter answer the questions found and implement the corresponding exercise suggestions into your daily life. Start now with week one.

Remember, you should always consult with a physician before beginning an exercise program.

Chapter/Week One
Exercise Preparation Work

1. Purchase a small calendar if you don't already have one and determine and schedule what days and at what time you are going to exercise.

2. Determine whether you are going to workout at home or in a public gym or studio atmosphere.

3. If you are going to work out at home you will at least need an exercise ball and a range of small dumbbells. Most women can get good workouts with dumbbells ranging from 5 to 12 pounds. Men will need to go up to 30- to 35 pounds (at the very least) or choose the exercises on the CD-Rom that use their body weight as resistance.

4. If you are going to work out in a fitness facility, from a price perspective and a hassle free customer transaction experience I recommend the YMCA or YWCA in your community.

5. Make sure you have the proper loose fitting exercise clothes and footwear. If you haven't worked out for a long time clothing is important because you don't want to be self-conscious when you begin your workouts in public.

6. Make sure that you have a lunch cooler and water bottle so that you can prepare your healthy food selections to take with you to school or work as well as so you can monitor the quantity of water you are drinking.

The Cross Roads Review

1. What are the four cross roads that lead to greater physical and spiritual health?

    _____

    _____

    _____

2. List the types of cardio you think you would enjoy and have the access and capability to perform.

    _____

    _____

    _____

3. List the spiritual areas of your life where you need to practice resistance training. Examples could include, smoking, drinking sodas or diet soda, abstaining from sexual promiscuity etc.

    _____

    _____

    _____

4. List the foods in red and state why they are red.

    _____

    _____

    _____

5. List the spiritual term that reflects the physical cross road of flexibility and how you intend to stretch it in your life.

    _____

    _____

    _____

    _____

Workout 1

Always: Warm-up with an eight- ten minute light cardiovascular exercise of choice, then start with a warm-up set using fifty percent of what you will be lifting on your first set and also stretch between sets. Fill in the chart below by selecting an exercise from each muscle group and filling in the pounds you lifted for each repetition.

(Choose one)

Exercises	Reps	Lbs.	Rest (Min.)
THIGHS (P)			
Leg Press	Set 1: 13-15	_____	1
Squats	Set 2: 10-12	_____	1
Leg Extensions	Set 3: 8-10	_____	1
Stationary Lunge	Set 4: 6-8	_____	1
Step Ups	Set 5: 20	_____	0
Ball Squat			
Other_____			
CORE ABS			
Flat Crunch	_____		0.5
Twist Floor Crunch			
Incline Crunch			
Leg Raise			
Twisting Ball Crunch			
Ball Rollouts			
Other_____			
CHEST (P)			
Flat Bench Press	Set 1: 13-15	_____	1
Incline Bench Press	Set 2: 10-12	_____	1
Machine Press	Set 3: 8-10	_____	1
Dumbbell Fly	Set 4: 6-8	_____	1
Push Ups	Set 5: 20	_____	0
Dumbbell/Ball Press			
Dumbbell/Ball Fly			
Other_____			

Page 1

45

Workout 1

(Choose one)

Exercises	Reps	Lbs.	Rest (Min.)
CORE ABS			
Flat Crunch	_____		0.5
Twist Floor Crunch			
Incline Crunch			
Leg Raise			
Twisting Ball Crunch			
Ball Rollouts			
Other_____			
SHOULDERS (S)			
Dumbbell Press	Set 1: 13-15	_____	1
Machine Press	Set 2: 10-12	_____	1
Dumbbell Side Raise	Set 3: 8-10	_____	1
Dumbbell Rear Squeeze	Set 4: 6-8	_____	1
Dumbbell/Ball Press	Set 5: 20	_____	0
Band Side Raise			
Other_____			
CORE ABS			
Flat Crunch	_____		0.5
Twist Floor Crunch			
Incline Crunch			
Leg Raise			
Twisting Ball Crunch			
Ball Rollouts			
Other_____			
TRICEPS- ARMS (S)			
Tricep Pushdown	Set 1: 13-15	_____	1
French Curls	Set 2: 10-12	_____	1
Rope Pushdowns	Set 3: 8-10	_____	1
One Arm Pushdowns	Set 4: 6-8	_____	1
Chair Dips	Set 5: 20	_____	0
Dumbbell/Ball Kickbacks			
Other_____			

Page 2

Workout 2

Always: Warm-up with an eight- ten minute light cardiovascular exercise of choice, then start with a warm-up set using fifty percent of what you will be lifting on your first set and also stretch between sets. Fill in the chart below by selecting an exercise from each muscle group and filling in the pounds you lifted for each repetition.

(Choose one)

Exercises	Reps	Lbs.	Rest (Min.)
BACK OF THIGH (P)			
Laying Leg Curls	Set 1: 13-15	_____	1
Dumbbell Dead Lifts	Set 2: 10-12	_____	1
Reverse Lunge	Set 3: 8-10	_____	1
Stationary Lunge	Set 4: 6-8	_____	1
Ball Curls	Set 5: 20	_____	0
Dumbbell Leg Curls			
Other_____			
CORE ABS			
Flat Crunch		_____	0.5
Twist Floor Crunch			
Incline Crunch			
Leg Raise			
Twisting Ball Crunch			
Ball Rollouts			
Other_____			
CALVES (P)			
Standing Raise	Set 1: 13-15	_____	1
Seated Raise	Set 2: 10-12	_____	1
Leg Press	Set 3: 8-10	_____	1
One Leg Raise	Set 4: 6-8	_____	1
Two Leg Dumbbell Raise	Set 5: 20	_____	0
Other_____			

Page 1

47

Workout 2

(Choose one)

Exercises	Reps	Lbs.	Rest (Min.)
CORE ABS			
Flat Crunch	_____		0.5
Twist Floor Crunch			
Incline Crunch			
Leg Raise			
Twisting Ball Crunch			
Ball Rollouts			
Other_____			
BACK (P)			
Straight Bar Pull Down	Set 1: 13-15	_____	1
Close Grip Pull	Set 2: 10-12	_____	1
Seated Row	Set 3: 8-10	_____	1
Reverse Grip Pull Down	Set 4: 6-8	_____	1
Dumbbell Row	Set 5: 20	_____	0
Band/Desk Row			
Two Arm Dumbbell Row			
Other_____			
CORE ABS			
Flat Crunch	_____		0.5
Twist Floor Crunch			
Incline Crunch			
Leg Raise			
Twisting Ball Crunch			
Ball Rollouts			
Other_____			
BICEPS- ARMS (S)			
Dumbbell Curl	Set 1: 13-15	_____	1
Barbell Curls	Set 2: 10-12	_____	1
Barbell Preacher Curls	Set 3: 8-10	_____	1
Dumbbell Hammer Curl	Set 4: 6-8	_____	1
Dumbbell/Ball Seated Curl	Set 5: 20	_____	0
Dumbbell/Ball Preacher Curl			
Other_____			

Page 2

48

Workout 1

Always: Warm-up with an eight- ten minute light cardiovascular exercise of choice, then start with a warm-up set using fifty percent of what you will be lifting on your first set and also stretch between sets. Fill in the chart below by selecting an exercise from each muscle group and filling in the pounds you lifted for each repetition.

(Choose one)

Exercises	Reps	Lbs.	Rest (Min.)
THIGHS (P)			
Leg Press	Set 1: 13-15	_____	1
Squats	Set 2: 10-12	_____	1
Leg Extensions	Set 3: 8-10	_____	1
Stationary Lunge	Set 4: 6-8	_____	1
Step Ups	Set 5: 20	_____	0
Ball Squat			
Other_____			
CORE ABS			
Flat Crunch	_____		0.5
Twist Floor Crunch			
Incline Crunch			
Leg Raise			
Twisting Ball Crunch			
Ball Rollouts			
Other_____			
CHEST (P)			
Flat Bench Press	Set 1: 13-15	_____	1
Incline Bench Press	Set 2: 10-12	_____	1
Machine Press	Set 3: 8-10	_____	1
Dumbbell Fly	Set 4: 6-8	_____	1
Push Ups	Set 5: 20	_____	0
Dumbbell/Ball Press			
Dumbbell/Ball Fly			
Other_____			

Page 1

49

Workout 1

(Choose one)

Exercises	Reps	Lbs.	Rest (Min.)
CORE ABS			
Flat Crunch	_____		0.5
Twist Floor Crunch			
Incline Crunch			
Leg Raise			
Twisting Ball Crunch			
Ball Rollouts			
Other_____			
SHOULDERS (S)			
Dumbbell Press	Set 1: 13-15	_____	1
Machine Press	Set 2: 10-12	_____	1
Dumbbell Side Raise	Set 3: 8-10	_____	1
Dumbbell Rear Squeeze	Set 4: 6-8	_____	1
Dumbbell/Ball Press	Set 5: 20	_____	0
Band Side Raise			
Other_____			
CORE ABS			
Flat Crunch	_____		0.5
Twist Floor Crunch			
Incline Crunch			
Leg Raise			
Twisting Ball Crunch			
Ball Rollouts			
Other_____			
TRICEPS- ARMS (S)			
Tricep Pushdown	Set 1: 13-15	_____	1
French Curls	Set 2: 10-12	_____	1
Rope Pushdowns	Set 3: 8-10	_____	1
One Arm Pushdowns	Set 4: 6-8	_____	1
Chair Dips	Set 5: 20	_____	0
Dumbbell/Ball Kickbacks			
Other_____			

Page 2

Cardio

Cardiovascular Exercise
Do your cardio three to five times a week.
(Choose one)
Bike; Bleachers; Elliptical; Sprints; Track; Treadmill; Other
Time / Duration:
MPH (speed):
Level:
Target Heart Rate:
 # Of Bleachers / Sprints:

Cardiovascular Exercise
Do your cardio three to five times a week.
(Choose one)
Bike; Bleachers; Elliptical; Sprints; Track; Treadmill; Other
Time / Duration:
MPH (speed):
Level:
Target Heart Rate:
 # Of Bleachers / Sprints:

Cardiovascular Exercise
Do your cardio three to five times a week.
(Choose one)
Bike; Bleachers; Elliptical; Sprints; Track; Treadmill; Other
Time / Duration:
MPH (speed):
Level:
Target Heart Rate:
 # Of Bleachers / Sprints:

Page 1

51

Cardio

Cardiovascular Exercise
Do your cardio three to five times a week.
(Choose one)
Bike; Bleachers; Elliptical; Sprints; Track; Treadmill; Other
Time / Duration:
MPH (speed):
Level:
Target Heart Rate:
 # Of Bleachers / Sprints:

Cardiovascular Exercise
Do your cardio three to five times a week.
(Choose one)
Bike; Bleachers; Elliptical; Sprints; Track; Treadmill; Other
Time / Duration:
MPH (speed):
Level:
Target Heart Rate:
 # Of Bleachers / Sprints:

Page 2

52

Chapter Two

The New (and Final) Covenant

This is the covenant I will make with the house of Israel after that time, declares the Lord. I will put my laws in their minds and write them on their hearts. I will be their God, and they will be my people.

Hebrews 8:10

First things first. You need to understand that the nature of God's relationship with man is dependent on a covenant, the New Covenant. Secondly, it is necessary for you to make a covenant with God regarding your health. But in order to do that you need to first understand what a covenant actually is. The term covenant actually refers to a binding agreement or a legal contract. Throughout the Hebrew Testament and into the New Testament we have records of God's various covenants with man.

There is the covenant that God made with Noah as He showed him a rainbow after the flood had stopped. It was a sign that God was putting his "Bow" down and a promise that He would never destroy the Earth by flooding again. In Christianity the rainbow is the pardon, the reconciliation between God and humanity. In ancient Christian symbolism the rainbow's principal colors are red, blue and green for fire, flood and earth. The rainbow is also our reminder that God is a God of Covenants.

While each of us has a universal covenant with God we also can have individual covenants with God. For example, in the Catholic Faith, many believers vow to surrender a habit or sacrifice particular comforts during the time of lent. I myself have made individual covenants with God as a way to remind me to continually follow many of the laws He has established for my own welfare and protection.

The great thing about God and covenants with Him is that He keeps His Word even when man does not. Through out the Hebrew Testament God made covenants with the nation of Israel as well as with specific individuals. Six of those covenants were made with Noah, Abraham, Isaac, Jacob, Moses, and David. Each of these great men in one way or another disappointed God by not following His instructions. Nevertheless, God fulfilled His covenant agreements with them.

Realizing their failures as well as our own, we are reminded of God's sovereign pre-destined plan of salvation and His love for us. We see the proof of His love when we read, *But God found fault with the people and said: "The time is coming, declares the Lord, when I will make **a new covenant** with the house of Israel and with the house of Judah. It will not be like the covenant I made with their forefathers when I took them by the hand to lead them out of Egypt, because they did not remain faithful to my covenant, and I turned away from them, declares the Lord.* (Hebrews 8:8-9)

And that new and seventh covenant did indeed come in the form of His Son, Jesus Christ. Note that it was the seventh covenant with a man and seven is the perfect number just as Christ was the perfect man!

For this reason Christ is the mediator of a new covenant, that those who are called may receive the promised eternal inheritance--now that he has died as a ransom to set them free from the sins committed under the first covenant. (Hebrews 9:15)

Are you getting it? We know from history that man can not keep his covenants and thus is doomed for failure without God being a part of them. How many times have you told yourself you were going to start eating right and exercising only to find that you could not do it on your own? If we go to God for forgiveness of sin, and we go to God for healing, and we go to God for help with our financial needs, why would we not go to God with our exercise and nutrition needs? God would love to lead you out of the slavery of over eating or the slavery of inactivity and this book will show you exactly **how** He wants to do it. It's not about treadmills and protein bars. It's about the way you think, the way you feel, the things that have happened to you in the past. It's about your attitude, your motivation, and mostly importantly your relationship with God.

That is why we need to go on a physical **walk** with God. This journey won't be some quick run on the treadmill that gets you down to a size 4 overnight. God did not say I will run with my people, he said I will walk with my people.(Leviticus 26:12) When we are walking with God we can take the time to stop and look at the things He wants to point out to us. Many of us avoid the walk with Him because some of the things He wants to point out will be painful for us to look at or deal with. But suffering is a principle in this thing we call life. God showed us how to conquer suffering by faith and love on the cross. He also told us, to come after Him we must deny ourselves and pick up our own cross to follow Him. (Mark 8:34) Later in this book we will look at suffering and the significance of it. Maybe we'll be able to experience in our own lives what the early Christians experienced in theirs when they suffered with joy.

In addition to our covenants with God, all of us at one time or another enters into some type of covenant agreement with other people. The most common examples include marriage, employment agreements, and business contracts. Similar to Christ facing the ultimate consequence of death, in order to complete God's covenant, we too must face consequences to complete ours. We must also face consequences when we do not uphold our covenants.

What if God made an announcement one day and said…"Attention Christians, when I made the New Covenant with you through my Son Jesus Christ, I didn't realize how much sin debt you were actually going to run up and so now the deal is off." Or what if Jesus Himself didn't want to keep his oath with His Father when the pain set in from the beatings and flogging? There wouldn't be a New Covenant if Jesus hadn't experienced a personal and painful discomfort.

We have to keep our word at all costs because our word is our foundation just as God's Word was the foundation of the world. John 1:1 says, *In the beginning was the Word, and the Word was with God, and the Word was God.* This reflection by John clearly indicates that the Word is Jesus. The Word is the driving force of creation, the standard of holiness, the principle of reason that governs the world. To break a worldly covenant with another person in your life is a serious sin in God's eyes.
Broken covenants, inevitably by the Holy nature of God, set off a chain reaction of unseen, negative and consequential manifestations in the lives of those who broke the covenant. If you find that there are covenants in your life that you have abandoned or unfulfilled, it's never too late to seek forgiveness and do the best you can to restore them. God is a loving and forgiving God and we should be the same.

To give you a great example and end this chapter I'll share another story with you from the life of one of my former clients. For the sake of his family I will not use any names.

This particular gentleman had come to me and was already in pretty good shape. He was a little on the thin side because he ran five miles almost everyday of the year. When he first came to Healthy Images he believed it was to add a little body weight by putting on some lean muscle. Little did he know that he was led to Healthy Images for spiritual training as well.

You see, this man was married and had children but had been separated from his wife for seven years without getting a divorce. Although he had broken his vows and pursued various other relationships during that period, his wife remained faithful to their covenant. When ever I asked him why he didn't just get divorced he always used the children as his excuse, which was a pretty good one.

Nonetheless, after two years of training in our studio, being prayed for by our staff, being witnessed to by our staff, and hearing the Word of God several hours a week through normal conversations during his workouts...he became broken. The Lord came to him or sent "messengers" on several occasions and touched his life in away that led him to repentance. After seven long years, the man is now once again living at home and honoring his covenant to God and his wife. You too can do the same...

Chapter/Week Two
Spiritual Workout

1. Take a moment to reflect on your own personal life. Are you in covenant relationship with anyone? List all the people you are in covenant with.

_____

_____

_____

_____

_____

_____

_____

_____

2. Have you broken covenant with any of them? List who.

_____

_____

_____

_____

_____

_____

_____

_____

_____

_____

3. If so, what were the circumstances surrounding your decisions to break covenant? Was your decision based on anger, frustration or fear?

_____

_____

_____

_____

_____

_____

_____

_____

_____

_____

4. What have been the consequences of breaking covenant?

_____

_____

_____

_____

_____

_____

_____

_____

_____

5. What can you do to reconcile each of your broken covenants? Can you take a forgiving attitude or personally suffer to fulfill that covenant?

_____

_____

_____

_____

_____

_____

_____

_____

_____

_____

Your New (and final) Covenant with God

Create a covenant with God in the form of a letter or note. Make it personal and loving. Humbly confess your problems and your bad habits and ask God to help you change and overcome your circumstances. Make this the final time that you come to the cross and vow to stay on the cross roads to health. He will honor your vows and walk with you wherever you go. Here is an example covenant you can use.

Father, I now know what a covenant is. I had always heard of the New Covenant and new that Jesus was the New Covenant but I never put two and two together. Please forgive me for all of my broken promises and agreements and enter into a new and final covenant with me regarding my health.

You know what is in my heart. Change my heart if you have to. You know I desire to be healthy but the events and circumstances in my life have led me to false beliefs and I have often lived in denial. Help me to understand your scriptures when I read them. Show me how to apply your holy and healthy principles into my life. I accept your forgiveness, I depend on your grace, and I want you to lead me into the promise of health and prosperity which you swore to give. I am now ready to learn, to be patient, to be a disciple of your teachings, to be supportive of everyone around me, to be held accountable, and to suffer through any lessons I will face ahead of me in my physical walk with you. I will change my attitude to be like that of Jesus, and I will always tell the truth so that the truth will be known to me. I promise to view myself the way that you view me, in the healthy self-image you created me to be. I promise to be faithful to you in all the seasons of life, in the desert, the valleys, the plateaus, and especially the mountain tops. And lastly, I promise to build my body, my mind, my soul, and the church through the submission and obedience to your teachings. Please enter into this covenant with me and cause me to fulfill it in the name of Jesus.

_____

_____

_____

_____

Workout 2

Always: Warm-up with an eight- ten minute light cardiovascular exercise of choice, then start with a warm-up set using fifty percent of what you will be lifting on your first set and also stretch between sets. Fill in the chart below by selecting an exercise from each muscle group and filling in the pounds you lifted for each repetition.

(Choose one)

Exercises	Reps	Lbs.	Rest (Min.)
BACK OF THIGH (P)			
Laying Leg Curls	Set 1: 13-15	_____	1
Dumbbell Dead Lifts	Set 2: 10-12	_____	1
Reverse Lunge	Set 3: 8-10	_____	1
Stationary Lunge	Set 4: 6-8	_____	1
Ball Curls	Set 5: 20	_____	0
Dumbbell Leg Curls			
Other_____			
CORE ABS			
Flat Crunch	_____		0.5
Twist Floor Crunch			
Incline Crunch			
Leg Raise			
Twisting Ball Crunch			
Ball Rollouts			
Other_____			
CALVES (P)			
Standing Raise	Set 1: 13-15	_____	1
Seated Raise	Set 2: 10-12	_____	1
Leg Press	Set 3: 8-10	_____	1
One Leg Raise	Set 4: 6-8	_____	1
Two Leg Dumbbell Raise	Set 5: 20	_____	0
Other_____			

Page 1

62

Workout 2

(Choose one)

Exercises	Reps	Lbs.	Rest (Min.)

CORE ABS

Flat Crunch
Twist Floor Crunch   _____   0.5
Incline Crunch
Leg Raise
Twisting Ball Crunch
Ball Rollouts
Other_____

BACK (P)

Straight Bar Pull Down   Set 1: 13-15   _____   1
Close Grip Pull   Set 2: 10-12   _____   1
Seated Row   Set 3: 8-10   _____   1
Reverse Grip Pull Down   Set 4: 6-8   _____   1
Dumbbell Row   Set 5: 20   _____   0
Band/Desk Row
Two Arm Dumbbell Row
Other_____

CORE ABS

Flat Crunch
Twist Floor Crunch   _____   0.5
Incline Crunch
Leg Raise
Twisting Ball Crunch
Ball Rollouts
Other_____

BICEPS- ARMS (S)

Dumbbell Curl   Set 1: 13-15   _____   1
Barbell Curls   Set 2: 10-12   _____   1
Barbell Preacher Curls   Set 3: 8-10   _____   1
Dumbbell Hammer Curl   Set 4: 6-8   _____   1
Dumbbell/Ball Seated Curl   Set 5: 20   _____   0
Dumbbell/Ball Preacher Curl
Other_____

Page 2

63

Workout 1

Always: Warm-up with an eight- ten minute light cardiovascular exercise of choice, then start with a warm-up set using fifty percent of what you will be lifting on your first set and also stretch between sets. Fill in the chart below by selecting an exercise from each muscle group and filling in the pounds you lifted for each repetition.

(Choose one)

Exercises	Reps	Lbs.	Rest (Min.)
THIGHS (P)			
Leg Press	Set 1: 13-15	_____	1
Squats	Set 2: 10-12	_____	1
Leg Extensions	Set 3: 8-10	_____	1
Stationary Lunge	Set 4: 6-8	_____	1
Step Ups	Set 5: 20	_____	0
Ball Squat			
Other_____			
CORE ABS			
Flat Crunch	_____		0.5
Twist Floor Crunch			
Incline Crunch			
Leg Raise			
Twisting Ball Crunch			
Ball Rollouts			
Other_____			
CHEST (P)			
Flat Bench Press	Set 1: 13-15	_____	1
Incline Bench Press	Set 2: 10-12	_____	1
Machine Press	Set 3: 8-10	_____	1
Dumbbell Fly	Set 4: 6-8	_____	1
Push Ups	Set 5: 20	_____	0
Dumbbell/Ball Press			
Dumbbell/Ball Fly			
Other_____			

Page 1

Workout 1

(Choose one)

Exercises	Reps	Lbs.	Rest (Min.)
CORE ABS			
Flat Crunch	_____		0.5
Twist Floor Crunch			
Incline Crunch			
Leg Raise			
Twisting Ball Crunch			
Ball Rollouts			
Other _____			
SHOULDERS (S)			
Dumbbell Press	Set 1: 13-15	_____	1
Machine Press	Set 2: 10-12	_____	1
Dumbbell Side Raise	Set 3: 8-10	_____	1
Dumbbell Rear Squeeze	Set 4: 6-8	_____	1
Dumbbell/Ball Press	Set 5: 20	_____	0
Band Side Raise			
Other _____			
CORE ABS			
Flat Crunch	_____		0.5
Twist Floor Crunch			
Incline Crunch			
Leg Raise			
Twisting Ball Crunch			
Ball Rollouts			
Other _____			
TRICEPS- ARMS (S)			
Tricep Pushdown	Set 1: 13-15	_____	1
French Curls	Set 2: 10-12	_____	1
Rope Pushdowns	Set 3: 8-10	_____	1
One Arm Pushdowns	Set 4: 6-8	_____	1
Chair Dips	Set 5: 20	_____	0
Dumbbell/Ball Kickbacks			
Other _____			

Page 2

65

Workout 2

Always: Warm-up with an eight- ten minute light cardiovascular exercise of choice, then start with a warm-up set using fifty percent of what you will be lifting on your first set and also stretch between sets. Fill in the chart below by selecting an exercise from each muscle group and filling in the pounds you lifted for each repetition.

(Choose one)

Exercises	Reps	Lbs.	Rest (Min.)
BACK OF THIGH (P)			
Laying Leg Curls	Set 1: 13-15	_____	1
Dumbbell Dead Lifts	Set 2: 10-12	_____	1
Reverse Lunge	Set 3: 8-10	_____	1
Stationary Lunge	Set 4: 6-8	_____	1
Ball Curls	Set 5: 20	_____	0
Dumbbell Leg Curls			
Other_____			
CORE ABS			
Flat Crunch	_____		0.5
Twist Floor Crunch			
Incline Crunch			
Leg Raise			
Twisting Ball Crunch			
Ball Rollouts			
Other_____			
CALVES (P)			
Standing Raise	Set 1: 13-15	_____	1
Seated Raise	Set 2: 10-12	_____	1
Leg Press	Set 3: 8-10	_____	1
One Leg Raise	Set 4: 6-8	_____	1
Two Leg Dumbbell Raise	Set 5: 20	_____	0
Other_____			

Page 1

66

Workout 2

(Choose one)

Exercises	Reps	Lbs.	Rest (Min.)
CORE ABS			
Flat Crunch	_____		0.5
Twist Floor Crunch			
Incline Crunch			
Leg Raise			
Twisting Ball Crunch			
Ball Rollouts			
Other_____			

BACK (P)			
Straight Bar Pull Down	Set 1: 13-15	_____	1
Close Grip Pull	Set 2: 10-12	_____	1
Seated Row	Set 3: 8-10	_____	1
Reverse Grip Pull Down	Set 4: 6-8	_____	1
Dumbbell Row	Set 5: 20	_____	0
Band/Desk Row			
Two Arm Dumbbell Row			
Other_____			

CORE ABS			
Flat Crunch	_____		0.5
Twist Floor Crunch			
Incline Crunch			
Leg Raise			
Twisting Ball Crunch			
Ball Rollouts			
Other_____			

BICEPS- ARMS (S)			
Dumbbell Curl	Set 1: 13-15	_____	1
Barbell Curls	Set 2: 10-12	_____	1
Barbell Preacher Curls	Set 3: 8-10	_____	1
Dumbbell Hammer Curl	Set 4: 6-8	_____	1
Dumbbell/Ball Seated Curl	Set 5: 20	_____	0
Dumbbell/Ball Preacher Curl			
Other_____			

Page 2

67

Cardio

Cardiovascular Exercise
Do your cardio three to five times a week.
(Choose one)
Bike; Bleachers; Elliptical; Sprints; Track; Treadmill; Other
Time / Duration:
MPH (speed):
Level:
Target Heart Rate:
 # Of Bleachers / Sprints:

Cardiovascular Exercise
Do your cardio three to five times a week.
(Choose one)
Bike; Bleachers; Elliptical; Sprints; Track; Treadmill; Other
Time / Duration:
MPH (speed):
Level:
Target Heart Rate:
 # Of Bleachers / Sprints:

Cardiovascular Exercise
Do your cardio three to five times a week.
(Choose one)
Bike; Bleachers; Elliptical; Sprints; Track; Treadmill; Other
Time / Duration:
MPH (speed):
Level:
Target Heart Rate:
 # Of Bleachers / Sprints:

Page 1

Cardio

Cardiovascular Exercise
Do your cardio three to five times a week.
(Choose one)
Bike; Bleachers; Elliptical; Sprints; Track; Treadmill; Other
Time / Duration:
MPH (speed):
Level:
Target Heart Rate:
 # Of Bleachers / Sprints:

Cardiovascular Exercise
Do your cardio three to five times a week.
(Choose one)
Bike; Bleachers; Elliptical; Sprints; Track; Treadmill; Other
Time / Duration:
MPH (speed):
Level:
Target Heart Rate:
 # Of Bleachers / Sprints:

Page 2

69

Chapter Three

Patience

"For here or to go?"

Fast food drive throughs, one hour photos, lose weight fast, get rich quick…let's be real, our society as a whole is impatient and does not like to wait on anything. People expect to restore their neglected health overnight. They expect their disarrayed marriages to be restored instantly after years of neglect. Today's workers who have never sacrificed their time and money to start a business from nothing at all expect stock options and ownership before they will even hire on in a new position.

There are many catalysts for this socially debasing phenomenon of impatience. For example, there is technology. We've embraced technology because of the speed at which we can acquire things and information. We can download information at the stroke of our fingertips. We buy movie tickets in advance so we don't have to wait at the box office line. We can also buy our music, books, clothes and groceries on-line so that we don't have to wait in traffic, for parking spots, or in long lines at the store.

Then there's the media. We've got the E! Hollywood network telling us "it's good to be somebody famous", to have money, to be skinny and then our lives will be perfect. These false representations about life being care free and a free for all is making the other 99.9% of the people on this planet envious and anxious about why their lives do not look like the lives of the people they see on television. Everybody watching television sees the lifestyles of not only the rich and famous but also of the make believers. The end result is the media sets the standard of what happiness and success look like and the rest of us take off in hot pursuit to achieve and attain it.

Sure, the conveniences of technology are great and make our lives easier and sure it would be nice to not only meet all of your financial needs but to also have a surplus with nice luxurious comforts in life but I challenge you to look at the impact that "real time" convenience and the media is having on our patience, especially for those things in our lives that are beyond our control.

Some things are just predestined to move at a divine pace and when we can't alter that pace we find ourselves irritated or goaded and we often move on to something else because we are not willing to wait, which ultimately means we miss the blessing God wants to give us. To those with callous hearts who think that God is unfair or unjust in his methods because we have to wait on things, even if they are "good" things, the following is for you.

But do not forget this one thing, dear friends: With the Lord a day is like a thousand years, and a thousand years are like a day. The Lord is not slow in keeping his promise, as some understand slowness. He is patient with

you, not wanting anyone to perish, but everyone to come to repentance. God's seeming delay in bringing about the consummation of all things is a result not of indifference but of patience in waiting for all who will come to repentance.
(2 Peter 3:8)

Losing weight, getting stronger, increasing flexibility and increasing our endurance are all things in our lives that are destined to occur for the most part at a pre-determined pace. The average time that it takes for a sedentary person to completely transform their body is 12 weeks. That is only three months! People will let their bodies go for ten years or more and then expect them to be transformed in real time. Sorry people...you have to wait. If you can't wait for three months, in extreme cases six months to a year, then you're in desperate need of the following scripture. *Yet the Lord longs to be gracious to you; he rises to show you compassion. For the Lord is a God of justice. Blessed are all who wait for him!* (Isaiah 30:18)

Waiting is part of faith and I pray that you will understand the following. 1 John 1 says that God is light. Well, a scientific fact is that at the speed of light, **time comes to a stop**, meaning for light...there is no time! So, if God is light, He is not bound by time in the way that we are. One of His numerous physical analogous is...as *timeless* light!

The lesson here may not be jumping off the page at you, so I will give you an application. If you want to lose weight or receive some other type of blessing or restoration from God, you will have to move in God's timeless frame, at His timeless pace. The fastest way to get in pace with God is to do what He tells you to do, with loving and submissive obedience.

When we don't wait on God and get in a hurry, we create life altering circumstances that sometimes have serious consequences and even fatal ones. Let's look at two impatient people in the bible and how their impatience has affected world history even to this day.

God appeared to Abraham and promised him and Sarai a son even though they were both well beyond the age of child bearing. (Genesis 15:4) Some time had passed since the revelation of this promise and Sarai impatiently implied that God was not keeping his promise when she told Abraham, *"Go, sleep with my maidservant."* Sleeping with a maidservant was an ancient custom, (illustrated in Old Assyrian marriage contracts, the Code of Hammurapi and the Nuzi tablets) used to ensure the birth of a male heir.

You see, Sarai had become impatient and decided to solve the problem of her barrenness by herself. The end result was two nations were created through two sons instead of one nation being created through one son as God originally intended. Those two sons were Ishmael and Isaac and their births from different mothers caused jealousy and feuding. Even today their descendants, the Palestinians and the Jews are still violently feuding over the Promised Land.

When we're in a hurry and not willing to wait we make mistakes that not only affect us but others as well. Not to mention if we are anxious about our needs or wants we may compromise out of uncertainty, which is a lack of faith, or fear.

We can see that not waiting, when it comes to our health, can have serious consequences as well. Because the media has dictated that beauty and worth come from leanness, strength, and athleticism we have millions of people, teens and adults, men and women, taking unsafe substances that manipulate the body's natural chemistry with dangerous life threatening side affects. Look at the professional baseball league and the steroid scandal plaguing our sports and media. Or what about the drug phen-fen that millions of women took to lose weight but at the same time seriously damaged their hearts. What are we doing to ourselves?

In the sixth Psalm David cried out, *"My soul is in anguish. How long, O Lord, how long?"* How many of us can relate to this cry? At one time or another we all ask God that question and we all get the same answer. He promises us healings, blessings and transformation as we begin *walking* with Him. Each of us would do well to simply read the Hebrew Testament when we find ourselves engaged in drawn out efforts to overcome illness or achieve something extraordinary in our lives, like healthy bodies! You see God gives us the example of the Israelites whom He rescued from slavery and promised to give "the land of milk and honey". *So I have come down to rescue them from the hand of the Egyptians and to bring them up out of that land into a good and spacious land, a land flowing with milk and honey*—(Exodus 3:8)

As we read this story we find that this rescue and prosperity did not happen instantaneously. It took time. Moses had to jump through a series of hoops before this promise came to fulfillment. It is no different for us today. Over the years I have come to learn that God does work in mysterious ways and His time frames are much different than ours. Many times God will supernaturally transport us to the future giving us an idea...a vision...a revelation of where we are going professionally, financially or with our health. But then, all in an instant, as soon as our quiet time with God is over we are brought back into the present reality of our circumstances and we wonder how on earth are we going to accomplish what we just saw or get to where He just took us? It is during those times that it is easy to get caught up in wondering about the when's and how's so much that we don't even realize that God is slowly step by step and little by little making away for His promise.

We see proof of this again in the same story I mentioned earlier. *"The Lord your God will drive out those nations before you, little by little. You will not be allowed to eliminate them all at once, or the wild animals will multiply around you."* (Deuteronomy 7:22)

"Little by little" was the promise. And the last part of that scripture brings us to another very important point. God is a God of order as we can simply see from observing science and all of creation. You see God knows that certain things have to be accomplished. Certain things have to be lined up, put in place, and tested to ensure our welfare once His promise comes to fulfillment. Earlier in the story we even see God flat out tells His people that He is sending an angel ahead of them. *"See, I am sending an angel ahead of you to guard you along the way and to bring you to the place I have prepared."* (Exodus 23:20)

You see if certain things are not accomplished prior to us receiving the promises that God gave us it could actually be detrimental to our welfare. The best example I can give is that of a parent and their teenage child. Every parent eventually wants there teenager to be self sufficient and able to drive themselves where ever they need to be but this only happens through a process of maturity where foundations like trust, safety and responsibility are laid. You wouldn't just give your children the keys to a car with out first making them practice, then take drivers education, get their license, and make sure they are insured. You want to make sure their welfare is secure and protected to the best of your ability before you will consider blessing them with that awesome privilege and responsibility. The same is true with us as adults and our heavenly Father. He wants to make sure that we are ready, mature and safely protected on our physical walk with Him to our "promised land".

The bottom line is this. God has a "promised land" for you. The Promised Land is not just Jerusalem but also an analogy for the many, abundant and numerous blessings God has already prepared for you. Perhaps it is a promotion at work, a house for your family, a college education, a place in ministry, overcoming an illness, or having a leaner healthier body; I don't know what it is for you, only you and God do. But, I do know this, you need to wait on and with Him because...*Faithful is He who calls you, and He will bring it to pass.* (1 Thessalonians 5:24)

Chapter/Week Three
Spiritual Workout

1. List some areas in your life where you need to become more patient.

   _____
   _____
   _____
   _____
   _____
   _____
   _____
   _____

2. What are some reasons God wants you to patient?

   _____
   _____
   _____
   _____
   _____
   _____
   _____
   _____
   _____

3. Describe the last time you were impatient, how you dealt with it, and what the outcome of your attitude or behavior was?

   _____
   _____
   _____
   _____
   _____
   _____

4. What are some consequences you have had to face for not be patient in the past?

_____

_____

_____

_____

_____

_____

_____

_____

_____

5. Pick a scripture from Chapter 3 and write it down. Try to remember it and for sure meditate on it this week while you are working out and doing your cardio.

_____

_____

_____

_____

_____

_____

_____

_____

_____

Workout 1

Always: Warm-up with an eight- ten minute light cardiovascular exercise of choice, then start with a warm-up set using fifty percent of what you will be lifting on your first set and also stretch between sets. Fill in the chart below by selecting an exercise from each muscle group and filling in the pounds you lifted for each repetition.

(Choose one)

Exercises	Reps	Lbs.	Rest (Min.)
THIGHS (P)			
Leg Press	Set 1: 13-15	_____	1
Squats	Set 2: 10-12	_____	1
Leg Extensions	Set 3: 8-10	_____	1
Stationary Lunge	Set 4: 6-8	_____	1
Step Ups	Set 5: 20	_____	0
Ball Squat			
Other_____			
CORE ABS			
Flat Crunch		_____	0.5
Twist Floor Crunch			
Incline Crunch			
Leg Raise			
Twisting Ball Crunch			
Ball Rollouts			
Other_____			
CHEST (P)			
Flat Bench Press	Set 1: 13-15	_____	1
Incline Bench Press	Set 2: 10-12	_____	1
Machine Press	Set 3: 8-10	_____	1
Dumbbell Fly	Set 4: 6-8	_____	1
Push Ups	Set 5: 20	_____	0
Dumbbell/Ball Press			
Dumbbell/Ball Fly			
Other_____			

Page 1

Workout 1

(Choose one)

Exercises	Reps	Lbs.	Rest (Min.)
CORE ABS			
Flat Crunch	———		0.5
Twist Floor Crunch			
Incline Crunch			
Leg Raise			
Twisting Ball Crunch			
Ball Rollouts			
Other_____			

SHOULDERS (S)			
Dumbbell Press	Set 1: 13-15	———	1
Machine Press	Set 2: 10-12	———	1
Dumbbell Side Raise	Set 3: 8-10	———	1
Dumbbell Rear Squeeze	Set 4: 6-8	———	1
Dumbbell/Ball Press	Set 5: 20	———	0
Band Side Raise			
Other_____			

CORE ABS			
Flat Crunch	———		0.5
Twist Floor Crunch			
Incline Crunch			
Leg Raise			
Twisting Ball Crunch			
Ball Rollouts			
Other_____			

TRICEPS- ARMS (S)			
Tricep Pushdown	Set 1: 13-15	———	1
French Curls	Set 2: 10-12	———	1
Rope Pushdowns	Set 3: 8-10	———	1
One Arm Pushdowns	Set 4: 6-8	———	1
Chair Dips	Set 5: 20	———	0
Dumbbell/Ball Kickbacks			
Other_____			

Page 2

81

Workout 2

Always: Warm-up with an eight- ten minute light cardiovascular exercise of choice, then start with a warm-up set using fifty percent of what you will be lifting on your first set and also stretch between sets. Fill in the chart below by selecting an exercise from each muscle group and filling in the pounds you lifted for each repetition.

(Choose one)

Exercises	Reps	Lbs.	Rest (Min.)
BACK OF THIGH (P)			
Laying Leg Curls	Set 1: 13-15	_____	1
Dumbbell Dead Lifts	Set 2: 10-12	_____	1
Reverse Lunge	Set 3: 8-10	_____	1
Stationary Lunge	Set 4: 6-8	_____	1
Ball Curls	Set 5: 20	_____	0
Dumbbell Leg Curls			
Other_____			
CORE ABS			
Flat Crunch	_____		0.5
Twist Floor Crunch			
Incline Crunch			
Leg Raise			
Twisting Ball Crunch			
Ball Rollouts			
Other_____			
CALVES (P)			
Standing Raise	Set 1: 13-15	_____	1
Seated Raise	Set 2: 10-12	_____	1
Leg Press	Set 3: 8-10	_____	1
One Leg Raise	Set 4: 6-8	_____	1
Two Leg Dumbbell Raise	Set 5: 20	_____	0
Other_____			

Page 1

82

Workout 2

(Choose one)

Exercises	Reps	Lbs.	Rest (Min.)
CORE ABS			
Flat Crunch			0.5
Twist Floor Crunch	_____		
Incline Crunch			
Leg Raise			
Twisting Ball Crunch			
Ball Rollouts			
Other_____			
BACK (P)			
Straight Bar Pull Down	Set 1: 13-15	_____	1
Close Grip Pull	Set 2: 10-12	_____	1
Seated Row	Set 3: 8-10	_____	1
Reverse Grip Pull Down	Set 4: 6-8	_____	1
Dumbbell Row	Set 5: 20	_____	0
Band/Desk Row			
Two Arm Dumbbell Row			
Other_____			
CORE ABS			
Flat Crunch			0.5
Twist Floor Crunch	_____		
Incline Crunch			
Leg Raise			
Twisting Ball Crunch			
Ball Rollouts			
Other_____			
BICEPS- ARMS (S)			
Dumbbell Curl	Set 1: 13-15	_____	1
Barbell Curls	Set 2: 10-12	_____	1
Barbell Preacher Curls	Set 3: 8-10	_____	1
Dumbbell Hammer Curl	Set 4: 6-8	_____	1
Dumbbell/Ball Seated Curl	Set 5: 20	_____	0
Dumbbell/Ball Preacher Curl			
Other_____			

Page 2

83

Workout 1

Always: Warm-up with an eight- ten minute light cardiovascular exercise of choice, then start with a warm-up set using fifty percent of what you will be lifting on your first set and also stretch between sets. Fill in the chart below by selecting an exercise from each muscle group and filling in the pounds you lifted for each repetition.

(Choose one)

Exercises	Reps	Lbs.	Rest (Min.)
THIGHS (P)			
Leg Press	Set 1: 13-15	_____	1
Squats	Set 2: 10-12	_____	1
Leg Extensions	Set 3: 8-10	_____	1
Stationary Lunge	Set 4: 6-8	_____	1
Step Ups	Set 5: 20	_____	0
Ball Squat			
Other_____			
CORE ABS			
Flat Crunch		_____	0.5
Twist Floor Crunch			
Incline Crunch			
Leg Raise			
Twisting Ball Crunch			
Ball Rollouts			
Other_____			
CHEST (P)			
Flat Bench Press	Set 1: 13-15	_____	1
Incline Bench Press	Set 2: 10-12	_____	1
Machine Press	Set 3: 8-10	_____	1
Dumbbell Fly	Set 4: 6-8	_____	1
Push Ups	Set 5: 20	_____	0
Dumbbell/Ball Press			
Dumbbell/Ball Fly			
Other_____			

Page 1

84

Workout 1

(Choose one)

Exercises	Reps	Lbs.	Rest (Min.)
CORE ABS			
Flat Crunch	_____		0.5
Twist Floor Crunch			
Incline Crunch			
Leg Raise			
Twisting Ball Crunch			
Ball Rollouts			
Other_____			
SHOULDERS (S)			
Dumbbell Press	Set 1: 13-15		1
Machine Press	Set 2: 10-12	_____	1
Dumbbell Side Raise	Set 3: 8-10	_____	1
Dumbbell Rear Squeeze	Set 4: 6-8	_____	1
Dumbbell/Ball Press	Set 5: 20	_____	0
Band Side Raise			
Other_____			
CORE ABS			
Flat Crunch	_____		0.5
Twist Floor Crunch			
Incline Crunch			
Leg Raise			
Twisting Ball Crunch			
Ball Rollouts			
Other_____			
TRICEPS- ARMS (S)			
Tricep Pushdown	Set 1: 13-15		1
French Curls	Set 2: 10-12	_____	1
Rope Pushdowns	Set 3: 8-10	_____	1
One Arm Pushdowns	Set 4: 6-8	_____	1
Chair Dips	Set 5: 20	_____	0
Dumbbell/Ball Kickbacks			
Other_____			

Page 2

85

Cardio

Cardiovascular Exercise
Do your cardio three to five times a week.
(Choose one)
Bike; Bleachers; Elliptical; Sprints; Track; Treadmill; Other
Time / Duration:
MPH (speed):
Level:
Target Heart Rate:
 # Of Bleachers / Sprints:

Cardiovascular Exercise
Do your cardio three to five times a week.
(Choose one)
Bike; Bleachers; Elliptical; Sprints; Track; Treadmill; Other
Time / Duration:
MPH (speed):
Level:
Target Heart Rate:
 # Of Bleachers / Sprints:

Cardiovascular Exercise
Do your cardio three to five times a week.
(Choose one)
Bike; Bleachers; Elliptical; Sprints; Track; Treadmill; Other
Time / Duration:
MPH (speed):
Level:
Target Heart Rate:
 # Of Bleachers / Sprints:

Cardio

Cardiovascular Exercise
Do your cardio three to five times a week.
(Choose one)
Bike; Bleachers; Elliptical; Sprints; Track; Treadmill; Other
Time / Duration:
MPH (speed):
Level:
Target Heart Rate:
 # Of Bleachers / Sprints:

Cardiovascular Exercise
Do your cardio three to five times a week.
(Choose one)
Bike; Bleachers; Elliptical; Sprints; Track; Treadmill; Other
Time / Duration:
MPH (speed):
Level:
Target Heart Rate:
 # Of Bleachers / Sprints:

Chapter Four

Discipleship

"Come follow me I will make you fishers of men"

Yeshua

That is probably my most favorite verse in the entire bible. It reminds me of the following photograph of me and one of my sisters sitting in a boat on dry land just before a fishing trip with my Dad. It had to have been taken around 1976 which would make me three or four years old. Little did I know that just as my earthly father would teach me how to fish that someday my heavenly father would do the same.

Let's just hope I am a better fisher of men than of fish.

Discipleship is defined as embracing and assisting in spreading the teachings of another. As I think about the idea of discipleship it seems like a foreign concept in this high tech age of the new millennium we live in. It seems so archaic. You probably never thought of yourself as a disciple but when you think about it the reality is we are all disciples of something.

Most people are following the teachings and principles of the world. That means most people are buying into the fast food, high fat, high sugar diets that we learn from television. But the fact that you are holding this book right now tends to make me think that you are different than most people.

Have you ever thought of yourself as a disciple? Do you think because we wear Nikes and drives cars instead of wearing sandals and riding donkeys that we are any less of a disciple than John, Peter, or the other ten? Do you think because you are a stay at home mom, the CEO of a corporation or a plumber that you aren't or can't be a disciple? Discipleship of Jesus teachings, of Christianity, is not dependent on your age or occupation. You do not need to be apart of the clergy to be a disciple. If you follow the teachings of Christ then you are a disciple. If you follow the biblical teachings and principles in this book then you are a disciple of good health.

Discipleship is an important element in achieving and maintaining great physical and spiritual health. In fact, teaching others will help reinforce what you are learning and in addition to that it will help create a supportive environment. We talk about the importance of support in the next chapter but the two go hand in hand.

Now, if you are a Christian that has truly found joy, peace, rest, energy, vitality, forgiveness, grace, and unconditional love in your relationship with God, then you don't even need to go out of your way to be a disciple. As Jesus said, *"You are the light of the world. A city on a hill cannot be hidden. Neither do people light a lamp and put it under a bowl. Instead they put it on its stand, and it gives light to everyone in the house. In the same way, let your light shine before men, that they may see your good deeds and praise your Father in heaven.* (Matthew 5:14-16)

Most people who are active disciples of the Word absolutely love sharing what the Lord is doing in their life and what He is teaching them. If you are a Christian and you don't feel this desire then I would do some soul searching on why you wouldn't want other people to have what you have and know what you know. Maybe you're scared or intimidated by the secular world we live in. Perhaps you think you need to know bible verses. Or maybe you are not even aware of the fact that God wants you to be sharing your Faith in Him. Let me clear all that up right here. *Then Jesus came to them and said, "All authority in heaven and on earth has been given to me. Therefore go and make disciples of all nations, baptizing them in the name of the Father and of the Son and of the Holy Spirit, and teaching them to obey everything I have commanded you.* (Matthew 28:18-20)

There is no reason to be afraid. If you are in a relationship with Christ you have been given spiritual authority. That scripture above is your great commission. I am not a pastor, a priest or a rabbi with years of theological training. On the other hand you could say that I have been through God's school of hard knocks. You probably have as well. But the fact remains, the teachings that I am presenting here have come from a prophetic authority that God has given me. As Christians we all have *serious* power and authority if we choose to use it and develop it. We should not be intimidated by anyone or anything, not even death itself.

And as far as not knowing bible verses...so what! Lots of times when a Christian is dealing with a non-believer the last thing they want to do is quote a scripture. If a non-believer or casual Christian has never read the bible they aren't even going to understand what you are talking about and they'll probably label you as a bible thumper or a religious zealot. No, instead, as

Christians, we should be able to "reach out and touch someone" just by walking into a room. Our presence, our joy, our exuberance, our kindness, and the way we speak to people or help the stranger in need should be one of the daily ways that we "evangelize".

I will never forget the first time someone told me I was an "Evangelical Christian". I was like, "What is that?" I had no idea what that meant and the word evangelism seemed to have a negative connotation to it. So I looked it up and it said evangelism was the zealous preaching and dissemination of the gospel, as through missionary work. I thought, right on! I am an evangelist! I guess that makes me like Robert Tilton? I guess I need a television network and some donations to perpetuate my ministry. Wrong! I use simple everyday tools, experiences, and encounters to do my part.

So what about you? You are a Christian, you love God, you tithe, you go to service a couple times a week, you pray all the time...but you're still just not comfortable with the concept of discipleship. Then take it slow. I am not telling you to go stand on the corner and hand out tracks or scare people passing by with quoted scriptures from the book of Revelations about the lake of fire. Instead take it easy. Talk to your spouse, your children, a friend or co-worker about the healthy lifestyle changes you are making. Start by giving them the nutritional or exercise tips that you are learning in this book and if they receive them or implement them into their lives you can casually mention you learned those principles from the bible. It is a lot easier to ask someone to go for a walk or join you in a workout at the gym than it is to ask them to go to church. Remember the Lord promised you "little by little" and that promise will be the same for those you disciple too.

And if you do choose to exercise the authority you were given and you decide to share the Lord's spiritual or physical teachings with someone, make sure you are not just selling the idea of a particular religion or denomination with a set of doctrines and rules. While God's love and the redemption of the soul appeals to our emotions, religion simply appeals to our intellect. Christianity...the essence of connecting with God through His Son Jesus Christ is what is paramount and it should not be hindered by any man made institutional divisions. *Selah*

Now, another aspect of discipleship involves *discipline*. Discipline is actually the root word of discipleship and it has several meanings. One definition is of punishment intended to correct or train, while another is defined as a behavior resulting from disciplinary training; or self-control.

Regarding the first definition of corrective punishment, the nature of our health is brilliant in that by default our bodies discipline (punish) us naturally when we don't take care of them. For example, in an acute situation, if a person were to indulge in alcohol beyond a healthy limit, their body might respond with nausea and or a headache. In a chronic situation, if a person repeatedly eats a high saturated fat diet over a period of ten years their body might respond with heart disease. Each of these example responses is attempted forms of corrective discipline. Notice the word attempted. Some people never heed the corrective disciplinary signals their bodies give them. You will see clearly in a later chapter that there is a natural system of accountability and that disease is in fact a form of discipline that God created as a default to guide and regulate our behavior.

There is however an alternative to this corrective discipline. To avoid the often uncomfortable form of corrective discipline we need to make sure we discipline ourselves. If we can discipline ourselves it means we have self control; and we know Father God has a lot to say on that subject.

God wants all of us to learn about control. Now control is defined as "to exercise authoritative or dominating influence over." And since all of us are controlling by nature we have to make a very important distinction about what God says we are actually supposed to have control over. Many of us try to control our spouses, our children, our employees, our environments, and our schedules...things that are all _external_ to us. Sometimes we do that lovingly and sometimes we do that forcefully and to our own detriment. Either way; trying to control things external to us is self-defeating and an exhausting impossibility. As I casually flipped through the bible, actively looking for what God says to us about control I found one common and underlying theme in most of the verses. Why don't you read a few of them and see if you can see what I found before I tell you.

1 Peter 5:8
Be **self**-controlled and alert.

Titus 2:12
It (God's grace) teaches us to say "No" to ungodliness and worldly passions, and to live **self**-controlled,

Galatians 5:22-23
But the fruit of the Spirit is love, joy, peace, patience, kindness, goodness, faithfulness, gentleness and **self**-control.

Did you figure it out along with me? God did not tell us to be in control of our husbands, wives, children and employees...he told us to be in control of our**selves**. In fact, we are not in control of anything _but_ ourselves. There is a reason for this too and many of you are not going to want to hear this because, one, you may not understand it, and two, it may scare you, but the truth is the world is under the control of evil influence. If this wasn't a true statement, then why would you at certain times in your life, when you want to do something good, still end up doing something bad? We discussed that partially in the first part of the book and here is more on the subject. John partially explains the cause of this "phenomenon" to us when he writes; _we know that we are children of God, and that the whole world is under the control of the evil one._ (1 John 5:19)

Is that conspiratorial? Does that sound scary or depressing? It doesn't to me because I am in control of my emotions right now. I have peace because I know that the Spirit of God, His words, His love, His teachings, His promises, all those wonderful and joy filled things that come from the Spirit of God are at work in my life regardless of what is happening in the world around me.

Now let's get even more specific. How do we really get in control of ourselves? We don't do it by controlling our bodies, and we don't do it by controlling our habits...we do it by controlling our minds. Peter teaches us, *Therefore*, **prepare your minds for action**; *be* **self-controlled**; (1 Peter 1:13)

Again, in a later chapter we really look at self control of the mind in detail through our attitudes as well as principles for developing Godly attitudes but the thing you need to get right now is this; *your physical and spiritual success is going to be dictated by the thoughts and attitudes of your mind.* The above scripture is telling us that to really be self controlled (disciplined) our **minds** have to be prepared for action. And what does "action" encompass? It encompasses everything; our speech, our physical bodies, whether or not we drink, when and how much we eat, whether or not we smoke, and whether or not we are sexually pure. All of our physical actions first have to be prepared through our minds. So by default, if your mind is prepared, your body will follow and so will your habits. We already exercised this principle with the week one exercises. All of that was preparatory work that engaged our *minds* prior to our physical exercise.

I think at Healthy Images, we have been so successful, and able to help so many people change not only their bodies but also their entire lives because we have guided them to study the Word of God, which resulted in the changing of their minds which resulted in self control and discipline! When you meditate on the word of God, you cannot simultaneously dwell on the things of the world because they are totally contradictory. The world says be a glutton and do whatever feels good at the moment, but God says to be self-controlled, be disciplined, and be a disciple. If by your free will you will prepare and choose to constantly keep God's law in your mind the result will be peace for you no matter what your circumstances are.

Dan was about 40 years old when he started the *Physical Walk with God* in our studio last year. He was 320 pounds and had gained most of that weight buy adding 10 pounds a year over the last nine years. He lived a high stress life combined with a poor American diet and a sedentary lifestyle. His cholesterol was over 250 and his triglycerides were above 300. Dan was in bad shape. He traveled a lot for his job and had four small children at home with little time to devote to himself. It wasn't until he decided to make a commitment (covenant) that he began transforming his life. His testimony is below.

*"In the first five weeks of the program I lost 10 pounds and got my cholesterol and triglycerides under control. In about 15 weeks, I had lost 30 pounds; gained muscle mass, had greater energy for my work and family, and actually lost the cravings for fatty and sweet foods. I not only looked and felt better; I gained a greater confidence that I can do this. I also realized how gluttonous I was in the past which led to physical and mental laziness turning me into a person I never wanted to be. My physical transformation actually opened the door for a greater spiritual transformation. Recognizing my prior poor habits, I could see and feel the sinful stains on my soul. I felt a greater need to know and understand God's role for me here on earth and that while I had been successful in business and my family that there were still talents that I had that were not being used. They were being wasted and I was ignoring God's message to use my talents given to me by Him for a greater good. I realized that taking care of my body made me more in touch with who I am and the need to live a more purpose driven life. Through scripture and spiritual writings I now stay focused on the spiritual and human virtues which continue to enlighten me as to the person I want to be like most...Jesus. Having lost a total of 65 pounds and six inches off my waist I now make and have time for my family, health and work. I even have time to volunteer at a religious not-for profit helping the less fortunate in Dallas. The Healthy Images program has helped me stay focused and **disciplined** with my priorities."*

As a body of Christian believers we cannot wait any longer to get our minds cleared from all the emotional stress that affects our behavior. It has to happen today. In our great country many of us are like Dan used to be. We are overly focused on being developed economically, professionally and intellectuality, when what we lack but certainly need the most is greater emotional intelligence.

Our emotional intelligence, our state of mind, is what controls us. If we truly want peace of mind, freedom from addictions, improved health, better looking bodies and intimate relationships with our family, friends, and co-workers we have to be led by the Spirit of God. We have to be led by what the Spirit and Word of God say, which are one in the same. If we are not pursuing spiritual things we are not pursuing self control or discipline. I think Paul sums it up best, *"You, however, are controlled not by the sinful nature (of the world) but by the Spirit, if the Spirit of God lives in you.* (Romans 8:9)

So many times people lack discipline because of the wrong attitude which leads to three tiny but extremely powerful words, "it's too hard". That is a lie and the s**word** of God cuts to the truth.

Now what I am commanding you today is not too difficult for you or beyond your reach... See, I set before you today life and prosperity, death and destruction. For I command you today to love the LORD your God, to walk in his ways, and to keep his commands, decrees and laws; then you will live and increase, and the LORD your God will bless you in the land you are entering to possess. (Deuteronomy 30:11-16)

That was apart of Moses discourse to the children of Israel. He was basically saying, the bottom line is to love God and obey Him being *disciplined....because it is not too hard to do.* Part of obeying God includes walking in His principles both physically and spiritually, taking care of our bodies, our hearts, and our minds.

For some of us who were born with great genetics the physical requirements of that obedience is far easier than to those of us who were born with slower metabolisms, larger body types or physical challenges. None the less, we are all called to pursue and uphold the same principles. It is important to note that each of us also has different levels of physical ability. Whether you're a professional athlete that spends years in intensive training or whether you're a moderate exerciser, you will always be required to put forth the effort to acquire and maintain good physical health.

The other reason it is not too hard is because we have help; we are not alone. Our help comes from the Holy Spirit. Just

as Yeshua said, "*And I will ask the Father, and he will give you another Counselor to be with you forever...* (John 14:16)

When we are lying on the couch and we feel guilty because we're not using that membership we bought, *that is not our conscious*, it is the Holy Spirit telling us to get up and move. When we are eating that extra serving of whatever we're not supposed to be eating to begin with, and we feel that guilt set in, that is not our conscious either. It is the Holy Spirit counseling us.

In summary, remember, discipleship of others is important and necessary for you to do because it fortifies and reinforces your own discipline. And without our own discipline, we are all subject to being disciplined by the natural laws of the universe that govern our health. So from here on out its time! From this moment on you need to live a disciplined life filled without regrets or excuses. When your time here is over and done with, you want to be able to tell Father, "I had discipline and I used it to glorify you!"

Chapter/Week Four
Spiritual Workout

1. What does discipleship mean and why is it important to your physical and spiritual health?

_____

_____

_____

_____

_____

_____

_____

_____

2. With some leadership training, in what areas of ministry do you think you could effectively help (disciple) others in your church?

_____

_____

_____

_____

_____

_____

_____

_____

_____

3. Is there a friend or family member you can engage in your exercise program who isn't in a relationship with Jesus and whom you may be able to disciple? If so when and how can you engage them?

_____

_____

_____

_____

_____

_____

_____

_____

_____

_____

4. What are the two types of discipline and which one do you intend to be apart of your life?

_____

_____

_____

_____

_____

_____

_____

5. In what area of your life do you need to exercise the most discipline, both spiritually and physically?

_____

_____

_____

_____

_____

_____

_____

Workout 2

Always: Warm-up with an eight- ten minute light cardiovascular exercise of choice, then start with a warm-up set using fifty percent of what you will be lifting on your first set and also stretch between sets. Fill in the chart below by selecting an exercise from each muscle group and filling in the pounds you lifted for each repetition.

(Choose one)

Exercises	Reps	Lbs.	Rest (Min.)
BACK OF THIGH (P)			
Laying Leg Curls	Set 1: 13-15	_____	1
Dumbbell Dead Lifts	Set 2: 10-12	_____	1
Reverse Lunge	Set 3: 8-10	_____	1
Stationary Lunge	Set 4: 6-8	_____	1
Ball Curls	Set 5: 20	_____	0
Dumbbell Leg Curls			
Other_____			
CORE ABS			
Flat Crunch	_____		0.5
Twist Floor Crunch			
Incline Crunch			
Leg Raise			
Twisting Ball Crunch			
Ball Rollouts			
Other_____			
CALVES (P)			
Standing Raise	Set 1: 13-15	_____	1
Seated Raise	Set 2: 10-12	_____	1
Leg Press	Set 3: 8-10	_____	1
One Leg Raise	Set 4: 6-8	_____	1
Two Leg Dumbbell Raise	Set 5: 20	_____	0
Other_____			

Page 1

Workout 2

(Choose one)

Exercises	Reps	Lbs.	Rest (Min.)
CORE ABS			
Flat Crunch	_____		0.5
Twist Floor Crunch			
Incline Crunch			
Leg Raise			
Twisting Ball Crunch			
Ball Rollouts			
Other_____			

BACK (P)			
Straight Bar Pull Down	Set 1: 13-15	_____	1
Close Grip Pull	Set 2: 10-12	_____	1
Seated Row	Set 3: 8-10	_____	1
Reverse Grip Pull Down	Set 4: 6-8	_____	1
Dumbbell Row	Set 5: 20	_____	0
Band/Desk Row			
Two Arm Dumbbell Row			
Other_____			

CORE ABS			
Flat Crunch	_____		0.5
Twist Floor Crunch			
Incline Crunch			
Leg Raise			
Twisting Ball Crunch			
Ball Rollouts			
Other_____			

BICEPS- ARMS (S)			
Dumbbell Curl	Set 1: 13-15	_____	1
Barbell Curls	Set 2: 10-12	_____	1
Barbell Preacher Curls	Set 3: 8-10	_____	1
Dumbbell Hammer Curl	Set 4: 6-8	_____	1
Dumbbell/Ball Seated Curl	Set 5: 20	_____	0
Dumbbell/Ball Preacher Curl			
Other_____			

Page 2

103

Workout 1

Always: Warm-up with an eight- ten minute light cardiovascular exercise of choice, then start with a warm-up set using fifty percent of what you will be lifting on your first set and also stretch between sets. Fill in the chart below by selecting an exercise from each muscle group and filling in the pounds you lifted for each repetition.

(Choose one)

Exercises	Reps	Lbs.	Rest (Min.)
THIGHS (P)			
Leg Press	Set 1: 13-15	_____	1
Squats	Set 2: 10-12	_____	1
Leg Extensions	Set 3: 8-10	_____	1
Stationary Lunge	Set 4: 6-8	_____	1
Step Ups	Set 5: 20	_____	0
Ball Squat			
Other_____			
CORE ABS			
Flat Crunch		_____	0.5
Twist Floor Crunch			
Incline Crunch			
Leg Raise			
Twisting Ball Crunch			
Ball Rollouts			
Other_____			
CHEST (P)			
Flat Bench Press	Set 1: 13-15	_____	1
Incline Bench Press	Set 2: 10-12	_____	1
Machine Press	Set 3: 8-10	_____	1
Dumbbell Fly	Set 4: 6-8	_____	1
Push Ups	Set 5: 20	_____	0
Dumbbell/Ball Press			
Dumbbell/Ball Fly			
Other_____			

Page 1

Workout 1

(Choose one)

Exercises	Reps	Lbs.	Rest (Min.)
CORE ABS			
Flat Crunch	———		0.5
Twist Floor Crunch			
Incline Crunch			
Leg Raise			
Twisting Ball Crunch			
Ball Rollouts			
Other_____			
SHOULDERS (S)			
Dumbbell Press	Set 1: 13-15	———	1
Machine Press	Set 2: 10-12	———	1
Dumbbell Side Raise	Set 3: 8-10	———	1
Dumbbell Rear Squeeze	Set 4: 6-8	———	1
Dumbbell/Ball Press	Set 5: 20	———	0
Band Side Raise			
Other_____			
CORE ABS			
Flat Crunch	———		0.5
Twist Floor Crunch			
Incline Crunch			
Leg Raise			
Twisting Ball Crunch			
Ball Rollouts			
Other_____			
TRICEPS- ARMS (S)			
Tricep Pushdown	Set 1: 13-15	———	1
French Curls	Set 2: 10-12	———	1
Rope Pushdowns	Set 3: 8-10	———	1
One Arm Pushdowns	Set 4: 6-8	———	1
Chair Dips	Set 5: 20	———	0
Dumbbell/Ball Kickbacks			
Other_____			

Page 2

105

Workout 2

Always: Warm-up with an eight- ten minute light cardiovascular exercise of choice, then start with a warm-up set using fifty percent of what you will be lifting on your first set and also stretch between sets. Fill in the chart below by selecting an exercise from each muscle group and filling in the pounds you lifted for each repetition.

(Choose one)

Exercises	Reps	Lbs.	Rest (Min.)
BACK OF THIGH (P)			
Laying Leg Curls	Set 1: 13-15	_____	1
Dumbbell Dead Lifts	Set 2: 10-12	_____	1
Reverse Lunge	Set 3: 8-10	_____	1
Stationary Lunge	Set 4: 6-8	_____	1
Ball Curls	Set 5: 20	_____	0
Dumbbell Leg Curls			
Other_____			
CORE ABS			
Flat Crunch		_____	0.5
Twist Floor Crunch			
Incline Crunch			
Leg Raise			
Twisting Ball Crunch			
Ball Rollouts			
Other_____			
CALVES (P)			
Standing Raise	Set 1: 13-15	_____	1
Seated Raise	Set 2: 10-12	_____	1
Leg Press	Set 3: 8-10	_____	1
One Leg Raise	Set 4: 6-8	_____	1
Two Leg Dumbbell Raise	Set 5: 20	_____	0
Other_____			

Page 1

Workout 2

(Choose one)

Exercises	Reps	Lbs.	Rest (Min.)
CORE ABS			
Flat Crunch	_____		0.5
Twist Floor Crunch			
Incline Crunch			
Leg Raise			
Twisting Ball Crunch			
Ball Rollouts			
Other_____			
BACK (P)			
Straight Bar Pull Down	Set 1: 13-15	_____	1
Close Grip Pull	Set 2: 10-12	_____	1
Seated Row	Set 3: 8-10	_____	1
Reverse Grip Pull Down	Set 4: 6-8	_____	1
Dumbbell Row	Set 5: 20	_____	0
Band/Desk Row			
Two Arm Dumbbell Row			
Other_____			
CORE ABS			
Flat Crunch	_____		0.5
Twist Floor Crunch			
Incline Crunch			
Leg Raise			
Twisting Ball Crunch			
Ball Rollouts			
Other_____			
BICEPS- ARMS (S)			
Dumbbell Curl	Set 1: 13-15	_____	1
Barbell Curls	Set 2: 10-12	_____	1
Barbell Preacher Curls	Set 3: 8-10	_____	1
Dumbbell Hammer Curl	Set 4: 6-8	_____	1
Dumbbell/Ball Seated Curl	Set 5: 20	_____	0
Dumbbell/Ball Preacher Curl			
Other_____			

Page 2

Cardio

Cardiovascular Exercise
Do your cardio three to five times a week.
(Choose one)
Bike; Bleachers; Elliptical; Sprints; Track; Treadmill; Other
Time / Duration:
MPH (speed):
Level:
Target Heart Rate:
 # Of Bleachers / Sprints:

Cardiovascular Exercise
Do your cardio three to five times a week.
(Choose one)
Bike; Bleachers; Elliptical; Sprints; Track; Treadmill; Other
Time / Duration:
MPH (speed):
Level:
Target Heart Rate:
 # Of Bleachers / Sprints:

Cardiovascular Exercise
Do your cardio three to five times a week.
(Choose one)
Bike; Bleachers; Elliptical; Sprints; Track; Treadmill; Other
Time / Duration:
MPH (speed):
Level:
Target Heart Rate:
 # Of Bleachers / Sprints:

Page 1

Cardio

Cardiovascular Exercise
Do your cardio three to five times a week.
(Choose one)
Bike; Bleachers; Elliptical; Sprints; Track; Treadmill; Other
Time / Duration:
MPH (speed):
Level:
Target Heart Rate:
 # Of Bleachers / Sprints:

Cardiovascular Exercise
Do your cardio three to five times a week.
(Choose one)
Bike; Bleachers; Elliptical; Sprints; Track; Treadmill; Other
Time / Duration:
MPH (speed):
Level:
Target Heart Rate:
 # Of Bleachers / Sprints:

Chapter Five

Support

"Stand by Me"

Do you remember the movie *Stand by Me?* The 1986 film was set in a small Oregon town, where a group of friends Gordie, Chris, Teddy, and Vern, were in search of a missing teenager's body. The four boys were played brilliantly by Wil Wheaton, Jerry O'Connell (Coosh from Jerry Maguire), Corey Feldman and the late River Phoenix. Wanting to be heroes for their hometown, they set out on an unforgettable two-day journey that turned into an odyssey of self-discovery. They snuck smokes, told tall tales, and stuck together when the going got tough. When they stumbled across one of their older brothers and his buddies, the town's knife wielding hoods who were also after the missing body, the boys discovered a strength they never knew they had; a strength that could only come from standing by one another.

I think this movie's heart tugging appeal, which mesmerizes a span of audiences from all generations, comes from the fact that everyone of us has a deep-rooted desire to be in fellowship with other people. At the root of the friendship that these boys possess we find an unconditional love regardless of their individual problems and circumstances and regardless of the tough external shells and egos that they tended to display for one another. I would even say that this fellowship, this love, this friendship is the basis of Christianity as we are all called to stand by God and one another.

In the book of Acts we find an account of a crippled beggar who for his entire life lay outside of the temple gates asking for money as God's people walked by him until one day when John and Peter came along. The story picks up here and goes like this;

When he saw Peter and John about to enter, he asked them for money. Peter looked straight at him, as did John. Then Peter said, "Look at us!" So the man gave them his attention, expecting to get something from them. Then Peter said, "Silver or gold I do not have, but what I have I give you. In the name of Jesus Christ of Nazareth, walk." Taking him by the right hand, he helped him up, and instantly the man's feet and ankles became strong. He jumped to his feet and began to walk. Then he went with them into the temple courts, walking and jumping, and praising God. (Acts3:3-8)

There is incredible insight in this scripture as to how we are to stand by one another in each other's time of need. The first thing Peter did was he looked at the man and exclaimed for the man to look back at him. During this process he didn't just observe this guy casually, listening to what the guy was asking for; he really truly looked at him and saw the man had a greater need. This man needed more than the money, he needed strength in his legs so he could walk. Many times in situations with our friends and families they maybe asking us for one thing but if we look closely at them and their situation we may find that they need something totally different, something more.

The same could be true for you. You may think you need to lose weight, but in reality you may need to deal with an emotion of bitterness or un-forgiveness before you can effectively do that. Almost every single person who has ever come to me for physical training, to lose weight, or change their lifestyle habits had a greater spiritual need to be dealt with first. When we are standing by someone we need to be sure that we truly look into their eyes and their souls and give them our full attention so that we can see what they truly need. The other great thing that Peter did in this story was he took this guy by the hand as he shared the name of Jesus Christ with him. He didn't just preach to this guy, he actually physically raised him up from his circumstance.

I can really relate to both the movie and this passage of scripture as I often times find myself in the role of standing by people. As a Kinesiologist, I stand by my clients, taking them by the hand, leading them through a maze of exercise equipment that they may never have had the knowledge of or courage to navigate by themselves. It is through this process that they become strong.

As Christians, we need to do the same thing for others. We need to not only share the Word of God with people but we also need to help them in their circumstances. *Suppose a brother or sister is without clothes and daily food. If one of you says to him, "Go, I wish you well; keep warm and well fed," but does nothing about his physical needs, what good is it?* (James 2:15-16) We have to stand by each other both spiritually and physically.

In addition to the movie, I also think of the famous song "Lean on Me". I know everyone remembers this song. The lyrics go like this;

Sometimes in our lives we all have pain
We all have sorrow
But if we are wise
We know that there's always tomorrow

Lean on me, when you're not strong
And I'll be your friend, I'll help you carry on
For it won't be long
'Til I'm gonna need somebody to lean on

Please swallow your pride
If I have things you need to borrow
For no one can fill those of your needs
That you won't let show

You just call on me, brother, when you need a hand
We all need somebody to lean on
I just might have a problem that you'll understand
We all need somebody to lean on

Lean on me, when you're not strong
And I'll be your friend, I'll help you carry on
For it won't be long
'Til I'm gonna need somebody to lean on

You just call on me, brother, when you need a hand
We all need somebody to lean on
I just might have a problem that you'll understand
We all need somebody to lean on

If there is a load you have to bear
That you can't carry
I'm right up the road
I'll share your load if you just call me
Call me — if you need a friend — call me

Bill Withers, 1972

You remember that song. I know its 30 years old and nobody listens to it anymore but people are always experiencing tough times and they need somebody to lean on. I see it everyday in my work place. People come into my studio with strong desires to lose weight. They have failed repeatedly, they are discouraged, and many times they just need to lean on somebody. It is my role to be that person that they lean on. And for the better part of the time, I can be there for them.

But in all honesty I too am human and cannot always support them the way they need to be. There are times when the business is wearing on me, my own health is distracting me, or my personal relationships with friends and family are preoccupying my thoughts. We are all human and as much as we want to always be there for each other, we sometimes fall short of that desire. Sounds depressing but we can take heart without fears or worries because God also wants us to lean on Him. *Trust in the Lord with all your heart and lean not on your own understanding;* (Proverbs 3:5)

This scripture above even tells us that in some cases, God does not want us to rely on ourselves or anyone else, but instead to rely on and be supported solely by *Him.*

I'll never forget the time the Lord told me specifically *"stand by me".* I was in a business situation with a fellow believer where I was being wrongfully slandered by him and was facing law suit threats that were totally unwarranted and founded on false testimony. We had gone to the pastors of our Church for mediation and even after I had been cleared by them of wrong doing the other believer continued with his claims. There was nothing else the pastors could do from that point on so I could not lean on them. I thought about leaning on an attorney, because in this particular situation I could have exercised my legal rights, and believe me I wanted to because there was $48,000 and the publishing rights to a book at stake, but the Lord specifically told me, *you will not have to fight this battle. Take*

up your positions; stand firm and see the deliverance the Lord will give you
(2 Chronicles 20:17)

Sure enough, I stood by the Lord as He told me to, and He delivered me from the persecution. Not only that, but He also blessed me beyond what I could have possibly imagined for me and those who were closely involved in that business. God wants the same for you. He wants you to lean on Him; He wants you to stand by Him as you go through this process of becoming healthier.

In many cases people are not in shape simply because they don't understand how the body works and the requirements that are necessary to get and stay in good shape. Perhaps God did not give you an understanding of health and fitness on purpose so that you would be dependent on a relationship with someone else for that knowledge. We will see in Chapter 12 that God has a body of believers and each one plays a role in that body. We all have a responsibility to seek out those people who have an understanding in areas of life that we do not. We are dependent on one another for sharing the gifts that God has given each of us. If you have failed previously at your health and fitness goals you should pray that God will place someone in your life to share with you the knowledge and wisdom to stand by you. He will do it.

On the other hand, there are people who **do** know what to do and have received the knowledge and understanding of the body but choose not to do anything with it. A great example of this is doctors who smoke. What is up with that? Perhaps these people do not trust the Lord as the proverb states. Not trusting God is the same as disbelief and it is an insult to the creator of your body. He knows how it works and if He has chosen to reveal that knowledge to you and you do not act on it then you are creating a barrier between you and Him as well as limiting what He wants to do for you in your life. You have to trust, you have to believe, *and most importantly you have to step out in Faith acting* on what you have been advised.

116

As the proverb states; we are to lean not on our own understanding but trust in the Lord. I challenge you today; if you need to lose weight, or if you are carrying a burden in your life, give yourself well deserved rest by leaning on the Lord and trusting that He will take the weight from you. He was sent to this world so that He might bear all of your weight. Give Him those extra pounds and burdens you're not supposed to be carrying. "Lean on the Lord" and "Stand by Me."

Chapter/Week Five
Spiritual Workout

1. Who in your life needs the most support from you right now? Do they need something other than what they are asking for? What are you going to do to support them?

    _____

    _____

    _____

    _____

    _____

    _____

    _____

2. In what areas of your life do you need the most support now and in addition to God, who can your turn to for support?

    _____

    _____

    _____

    _____

    _____

    _____

    _____

    _____

3. Write down Proverbs 3:5 and memorize it so you can meditate on it during your workouts and cardio this week.

    _____

    _____

    _____

    _____

_____

_____

_____

_____

_____

_____

4. In what areas of your life are you confused or dissatisfied and you need to lean on the Lord?

_____

_____

_____

_____

_____

_____

_____

_____

5. Are there any groups, bible studies, life teams or ministries at your church that you can join to get and give support? Write them down and considering joining one.

_____

_____

_____

_____

_____

_____

_____

_____

_____

Workout 1

Always: Warm-up with an eight- ten minute light cardiovascular exercise of choice, then start with a warm-up set using fifty percent of what you will be lifting on your first set and also stretch between sets. Fill in the chart below by selecting an exercise from each muscle group and filling in the pounds you lifted for each repetition.

(Choose one)

Exercises	Reps	Lbs.	Rest (Min.)
THIGHS (P)			
Leg Press	Set 1: 13-15	_____	1
Squats	Set 2: 10-12	_____	1
Leg Extensions	Set 3: 8-10	_____	1
Stationary Lunge	Set 4: 6-8	_____	1
Step Ups	Set 5: 20	_____	0
Ball Squat			
Other_____			
CORE ABS			
Flat Crunch		_____	0.5
Twist Floor Crunch			
Incline Crunch			
Leg Raise			
Twisting Ball Crunch			
Ball Rollouts			
Other_____			
CHEST (P)			
Flat Bench Press	Set 1: 13-15	_____	1
Incline Bench Press	Set 2: 10-12	_____	1
Machine Press	Set 3: 8-10	_____	1
Dumbbell Fly	Set 4: 6-8	_____	1
Push Ups	Set 5: 20	_____	0
Dumbbell/Ball Press			
Dumbbell/Ball Fly			
Other_____			

Page 1

Workout 1

(Choose one)

Exercises	Reps	Lbs.	Rest (Min.)
CORE ABS			
Flat Crunch	_____		0.5
Twist Floor Crunch			
Incline Crunch			
Leg Raise			
Twisting Ball Crunch			
Ball Rollouts			
Other_____			
SHOULDERS (S)			
Dumbbell Press	Set 1: 13-15	_____	1
Machine Press	Set 2: 10-12	_____	1
Dumbbell Side Raise	Set 3: 8-10	_____	1
Dumbbell Rear Squeeze	Set 4: 6-8	_____	1
Dumbbell/Ball Press	Set 5: 20	_____	0
Band Side Raise			
Other_____			
CORE ABS			
Flat Crunch	_____		0.5
Twist Floor Crunch			
Incline Crunch			
Leg Raise			
Twisting Ball Crunch			
Ball Rollouts			
Other_____			
TRICEPS- ARMS (S)			
Tricep Pushdown	Set 1: 13-15	_____	1
French Curls	Set 2: 10-12	_____	1
Rope Pushdowns	Set 3: 8-10	_____	1
One Arm Pushdowns	Set 4: 6-8	_____	1
Chair Dips	Set 5: 20	_____	0
Dumbbell/Ball Kickbacks			
Other_____			

Page 2

121

Workout 2

Always: Warm-up with an eight- ten minute light cardiovascular exercise of choice, then start with a warm-up set using fifty percent of what you will be lifting on your first set and also stretch between sets. Fill in the chart below by selecting an exercise from each muscle group and filling in the pounds you lifted for each repetition.

(Choose one)

Exercises	Reps	Lbs.	Rest (Min.)
BACK OF THIGH (P)			
Laying Leg Curls	Set 1: 13-15	_____	1
Dumbbell Dead Lifts	Set 2: 10-12	_____	1
Reverse Lunge	Set 3: 8-10	_____	1
Stationary Lunge	Set 4: 6-8	_____	1
Ball Curls	Set 5: 20	_____	0
Dumbbell Leg Curls			
Other_____			
CORE ABS			
Flat Crunch		_____	0.5
Twist Floor Crunch			
Incline Crunch			
Leg Raise			
Twisting Ball Crunch			
Ball Rollouts			
Other_____			
CALVES (P)			
Standing Raise	Set 1: 13-15	_____	1
Seated Raise	Set 2: 10-12	_____	1
Leg Press	Set 3: 8-10	_____	1
One Leg Raise	Set 4: 6-8	_____	1
Two Leg Dumbbell Raise	Set 5: 20	_____	0
Other_____			

Page 1

122

Workout 2

(Choose one)

Exercises	Reps	Lbs.	Rest (Min.)
CORE ABS			
Flat Crunch	_____		0.5
Twist Floor Crunch			
Incline Crunch			
Leg Raise			
Twisting Ball Crunch			
Ball Rollouts			
Other_____			

BACK (P)

Straight Bar Pull Down	Set 1: 13-15	_____	1
Close Grip Pull	Set 2: 10-12	_____	1
Seated Row	Set 3: 8-10	_____	1
Reverse Grip Pull Down	Set 4: 6-8	_____	1
Dumbbell Row	Set 5: 20	_____	0
Band/Desk Row			
Two Arm Dumbbell Row			
Other_____			

CORE ABS

Flat Crunch	_____		0.5
Twist Floor Crunch			
Incline Crunch			
Leg Raise			
Twisting Ball Crunch			
Ball Rollouts			
Other_____			

BICEPS- ARMS (S)

Dumbbell Curl	Set 1: 13-15	_____	1
Barbell Curls	Set 2: 10-12	_____	1
Barbell Preacher Curls	Set 3: 8-10	_____	1
Dumbbell Hammer Curl	Set 4: 6-8	_____	1
Dumbbell/Ball Seated Curl	Set 5: 20	_____	0
Dumbbell/Ball Preacher Curl			
Other_____			

Page 2

123

Workout 1

Always: Warm-up with an eight- ten minute light cardiovascular exercise of choice, then start with a warm-up set using fifty percent of what you will be lifting on your first set and also stretch between sets. Fill in the chart below by selecting an exercise from each muscle group and filling in the pounds you lifted for each repetition.

(Choose one)

Exercises	Reps	Lbs.	Rest (Min.)
THIGHS (P)			
Leg Press	Set 1: 13-15	_____	1
Squats	Set 2: 10-12	_____	1
Leg Extensions	Set 3: 8-10	_____	1
Stationary Lunge	Set 4: 6-8	_____	1
Step Ups	Set 5: 20	_____	0
Ball Squat			
Other_____			
CORE ABS			
Flat Crunch		_____	0.5
Twist Floor Crunch			
Incline Crunch			
Leg Raise			
Twisting Ball Crunch			
Ball Rollouts			
Other_____			
CHEST (P)			
Flat Bench Press	Set 1: 13-15	_____	1
Incline Bench Press	Set 2: 10-12	_____	1
Machine Press	Set 3: 8-10	_____	1
Dumbbell Fly	Set 4: 6-8	_____	1
Push Ups	Set 5: 20	_____	0
Dumbbell/Ball Press			
Dumbbell/Ball Fly			
Other_____			

Page 1

Workout 1

(Choose one)

Exercises	Reps	Lbs.	Rest (Min.)
CORE ABS			
Flat Crunch	____		0.5
Twist Floor Crunch			
Incline Crunch			
Leg Raise			
Twisting Ball Crunch			
Ball Rollouts			
Other____			

SHOULDERS (S)			
Dumbbell Press	Set 1: 13-15	____	1
Machine Press	Set 2: 10-12	____	1
Dumbbell Side Raise	Set 3: 8-10	____	1
Dumbbell Rear Squeeze	Set 4: 6-8	____	1
Dumbbell/Ball Press	Set 5: 20	____	0
Band Side Raise			
Other____			

CORE ABS			
Flat Crunch	____		0.5
Twist Floor Crunch			
Incline Crunch			
Leg Raise			
Twisting Ball Crunch			
Ball Rollouts			
Other____			

TRICEPS- ARMS (S)			
Tricep Pushdown	Set 1: 13-15	____	1
French Curls	Set 2: 10-12	____	1
Rope Pushdowns	Set 3: 8-10	____	1
One Arm Pushdowns	Set 4: 6-8	____	1
Chair Dips	Set 5: 20	____	0
Dumbbell/Ball Kickbacks			
Other____			

Page 2

125

Cardio

Cardiovascular Exercise
Do your cardio three to five times a week.
(Choose one)
Bike; Bleachers; Elliptical; Sprints; Track; Treadmill; Other
Time / Duration:
MPH (speed):
Level:
Target Heart Rate:
 # Of Bleachers / Sprints:

Cardiovascular Exercise
Do your cardio three to five times a week.
(Choose one)
Bike; Bleachers; Elliptical; Sprints; Track; Treadmill; Other
Time / Duration:
MPH (speed):
Level:
Target Heart Rate:
 # Of Bleachers / Sprints:

Cardiovascular Exercise
Do your cardio three to five times a week.
(Choose one)
Bike; Bleachers; Elliptical; Sprints; Track; Treadmill; Other
Time / Duration:
MPH (speed):
Level:
Target Heart Rate:
 # Of Bleachers / Sprints:

Page 1

126

Cardio

Cardiovascular Exercise
Do your cardio three to five times a week.
(Choose one)
Bike; Bleachers; Elliptical; Sprints; Track; Treadmill; Other
Time / Duration:
MPH (speed):
Level:
Target Heart Rate:
 # Of Bleachers / Sprints:

Cardiovascular Exercise
Do your cardio three to five times a week.
(Choose one)
Bike; Bleachers; Elliptical; Sprints; Track; Treadmill; Other
Time / Duration:
MPH (speed):
Level:
Target Heart Rate:
 # Of Bleachers / Sprints:

Chapter Six

Accountability

"Son, your ego is writing checks your body can't cash..."

From Top Gun

Hollywood often has a way of creating larger than life personalities in their illusory films making even the most arrogant of characters lovable. That was the case with "Maverick" in the 1986 film Top Gun. Tom Cruises' over inflated ego was very much affable as he flew a $38 million F-14 Tomcat at Mach 2 with 27,000 pounds of static thrust sitting between his legs. It didn't matter that he was breaking rules, living dangerously, and risking the safety of others; Hollywood made him look cool anyways.

That was Hollywood fiction but how many of us are actually like Tom Cruise in our own unique way? When it comes to your health and your relationships at home and work, are you writing checks your bodies can't cash?

For example; has your ego convinced you that you can get away with not working out for weeks, months or even years at a time? Is your ego trapping you in the glory days of your youth believing that there is a supernatural and residual effect from the workouts you once did 10 years ago?

What about your personal and professional relationships? Has your ego convinced you that you don't have to compromise in areas of communication with your spouse because you are the bread winner and the financial provider? Has your ego convinced you that you don't have to help with the raising of your children or help them with their school work because you worked your office gig all week? Or what about the company you signed on with accepting the responsibility of achieving specific objectives for the overall welfare of a body of individuals. Did your ego convince you that you were entitled to walk away from or blow off that professional commitment because things did not go according to your perspective? The truth is we are all "Mavericks" in our own way and we let our egos get in the way of what is best for ourselves and those around us.

When we look at our ego we can look at it several ways. In fact, ego is defined one; as an exaggerated sense of self importance and conceit, or two; as appropriate pride in oneself, or, self-esteem. I believe I highlighted the behavior that exemplifies the first definition with the tough questions I asked you to meditate on above. Let's look at the second definition of ego but from a Godly perspective.

Then Jesus came from Galilee to the Jordan to be baptized by John. But John tried to deter him, saying, "I need to be baptized by you, and do you come to me?" Jesus replied, "Let it be so now; it is proper for us to do this to fulfill all righteousness." Then John consented. (Matthew 3:13-15)

In this passage we see the ultimate suppression of ego as the Son of God humbled himself in order to be baptized by John. The effects of His humbling act were tremendous. It showed **support** for what John was doing; and it inaugurated his public ministry, as well as identified Christ, although perfect, with the penitent people who were watching. We need to stop and ask ourselves if our egos provide that same effect on those who are watching us. Do we show support for causes greater than ourselves with our words and our behavior? We all need to have some type of accountability as well as a model or standard to follow. I believe the following scripture is in fact the bottom line for all of us. Paul writes, *But by the grace of God I am what I am, and His grace to me was not without effect.* (1 Corinthians 15:10)

Paul of all people was a guy who had many reasons to boast. He could have boasted on his social status, his Jewish heritage, and his knowledge of the Hebrew testament. But in his writing, he humbly acknowledges the Truth that all of his prominence, success, and blessings were a result of God's grace on his life.

We need to be more like John the Baptist, we need to be more like Paul, no, we need to be more like *Christ*. The reason we need to check our egos at the door is because we will be held accountable for everything we say or do. We know this from the very beginning. All of our decisions have consequences. Adam and Eve's egos led them to the wrong food and their sinful indulgence resulted in their separation from God and ultimately their (our) death. Are you allowing the indulgence of unhealthy foods or the wrong quantity of food to separate you from God and His best life for you? Is your ego telling you that you will not be accountable either spiritually or physically for the misuse of your body, heart or mind? What about smoking, drinking excessive alcohol, or using illicit drugs? Okay, so you don't do any of that. Maybe you were born with great genetics, you don't over eat or use the substances I mentioned above, but are you exercising? Are you moving your body, are you setting an example for the unhealthy people around you? We are accountable not only for ourselves but also for our fellow man. *"And from each man, too, I will demand an accounting for the life of his fellow man."* (Genesis 9:5)

This goes back to the idea of support. We are all in this together, one body, one church! You can scour through the Hebrew Testament and in just about every book see where God was holding someone accountable for their actions or disobedience to His principles. Let me just highlight a couple.

In 1 Samuel 15:24 we hear King Saul tell Samuel the prophet the following, *"I was afraid of the people and so I gave in to them..."* Earlier in this passage Saul was specifically told by God's prophet to destroy everything that belongs to his enemies and to not spare anyone's life. Long story short, the people Saul was leading wanted to take plunders for themselves and for some reason they also spared the opposing King's life. This amounted to disobedience to the voice of God and as a result of that disobedience it cost Saul his leadership as King. Saul was all set to rule and be blessed forever as the king but his ego and disobedience to God's prophet led way for his demise and King David's great reign. Saul lost his position and authority. What do you stand to lose if you do not listen to me or follow the biblical principles outlined in this book?

Let me preface this next statement with the fact that I am humbled to be in God's service and writing this book, but He has made me His prophet for you in the area of your health. He is speaking to you through me, through this book, through His word and He expects you to respond to it. *If anyone does not listen to my words that the prophet speaks in my name, I myself will call him to account.* (Deuteronomy 8:19)

An even more specific example that relates directly to your health and being held accountable for your actions can be seen when God said, *"If you listen carefully to the voice of the Lord your God and do what is right in his eyes, if you pay attention to his commands and keep all his decrees, I will not bring on you any of the diseases I brought on the*

Egyptians, for I am the Lord, who heals you." (Exodus 15:26) Here God flat out promised that if people would obey him they would remain free from diseases.

Moses addresses the people again in Deuteronomy 28:58-61.

If you do not carefully follow all the words of this law, which are written in this book, and do not revere this glorious and awesome name–the Lord your God—59 the Lord will send fearful plagues on you and your descendants, harsh and prolonged disasters, and severe and lingering illnesses. He will bring upon you all the diseases of Egypt that you dreaded, and they will cling to you. The Lord will also bring on you every kind of sickness and disaster not recorded in this Book of the Law, until you are destroyed.

It sounds like hell fire and brimstone *but it's really not.* It's loving advice. According to verse 61, there were diseases that the children of Israel didn't even know about back then. But what about us today? We know a lot more about health and medicine than they did but we still ignore God's physical and spiritual principles. Take heart disease for example. We now know through science that smoking and certain foods cause heart disease but some people smoke and eat bad anyway.

Everything is exactly like God told us; there are consequences and we are held *accountable simply by disease.* Modern medicine has confirmed this. It is not like God furiously and hatefully sends an angel down to earth to strike someone with artery plaque every time they eat a cheeseburger. No, it happens by default. Disease and sickness is a default built into the world, into the environment. The potential for it is built into our bodies. If we follow the principles, genetics aside (generational curses through descendants- see verse 59 above), we are promised good health. If not, we are held accountable.

Even God's moral laws are designed to keep us healthy and free from physical sickness. Here's another example; following God's laws against adultery, prostitution, or sexual immorality would keep people free from venereal diseases. As human beings we are highly complex and all of the physical, emotional and spiritual

133

aspects of our lives are intertwined. Modern medicine is now even able to confirm what these laws assumed 4000 years ago. People couldn't diagnose or treat diseases back then. It is only through modern medical technology that we now can see that God's moral code and standard of "clean" living will in fact keep us not only spiritually healthy *but also physically healthy.*

So if accountability is so important how can we maintain it? Aside from our covenants, we can hold each other accountable or we can find someone to hold us accountable. I once asked one of my clients who had been working out with me for five years, "why do you keep paying me to work you out every week when I have already taught you everything you need to know about eating and exercise?" Her response was "Because I need the accountability. If you weren't here waiting on me I wouldn't do it on my own." It was that day and that statement that added value and understanding to the purpose God has for my life. I simply and humbly help Him hold people accountable.

Now everyone may not be as fortunate as that woman and may not be able to afford a personal trainer week after week and year after year so what else can you do for accountability? You can get a workout partner who will meet you for walks or bible study. You can get a friend from church to call you a couple times per week to quiz you verbally on how you're doing with your program.

Even better than that, my hope in writing this book is that churches will embrace *"A Physical Walk with God"* as a biblical study tool and encourage small group studies. Healthy Images can even help churches set up small fitness rooms on their campuses to further promote the ministry of healthy living. The physical health of our church leaders and members is crucial in carrying out God's will and therefore there has to be church wide accountability. We know this as the truth because Paul confirms it by writing, *"as surely as I live,' says the Lord, `every knee will bow before me; every tongue will confess to God.' "So then, each of us will give an account of himself to God.* (Romans 14:11-12)

Accountability is an essential component to achieving and maintaining great physical and spiritual health. So be sure to build it into all areas of your life!

Chapter/Week Six
Spiritual Workout

1. Does your ego interfere with your personal or professional relationships? With whom are you in conflict and what are the circumstances?

_____

_____

_____

_____

_____

_____

_____

_____

2. What can you do to suppress your ego and create humility and peace in your particular situation?

_____

_____

_____

_____

_____

_____

_____

_____

3. What scripture did Paul write that addressed ego and humility?

_____

_____

_____

_____

_____

_____

_____

_____

_____

4. What is the relationship between God's laws and your physical health and how can following them help you remain healthy?

_____

_____

_____

_____

_____

_____

_____

_____

5. Has your ego kept you from working out and thus you now suffer from poor health or are on the verge of it? What scripture/s can help keep you accountable to exercising and eating right? (you can even refer to chapter one if you need)

_____

_____

_____

_____

_____

_____

_____

_____

Workout 2

Always: Warm-up with an eight- ten minute light cardiovascular exercise of choice, then start with a warm-up set using fifty percent of what you will be lifting on your first set and also stretch between sets. Fill in the chart below by selecting an exercise from each muscle group and filling in the pounds you lifted for each repetition.

(Choose one)

Exercises	Reps	Lbs.	Rest (Min.)
BACK OF THIGH (P)			
Laying Leg Curls	Set 1: 13-15	_____	1
Dumbbell Dead Lifts	Set 2: 10-12	_____	1
Reverse Lunge	Set 3: 8-10	_____	1
Stationary Lunge	Set 4: 6-8	_____	1
Ball Curls	Set 5: 20	_____	0
Dumbbell Leg Curls			
Other_____			
CORE ABS			
Flat Crunch	_____		0.5
Twist Floor Crunch			
Incline Crunch			
Leg Raise			
Twisting Ball Crunch			
Ball Rollouts			
Other_____			
CALVES (P)			
Standing Raise	Set 1: 13-15	_____	1
Seated Raise	Set 2: 10-12	_____	1
Leg Press	Set 3: 8-10	_____	1
One Leg Raise	Set 4: 6-8	_____	1
Two Leg Dumbbell Raise	Set 5: 20	_____	0
Other_____			

Page 1

138

Workout 2

(Choose one)

Exercises	Reps	Lbs.	Rest (Min.)

CORE ABS
Flat Crunch
Twist Floor Crunch
Incline Crunch
Leg Raise
Twisting Ball Crunch
Ball Rollouts
Other_____

                  —————   0.5

BACK (P)

Exercise	Set	Lbs.	Rest
Straight Bar Pull Down	Set 1: 13-15	———	1
Close Grip Pull	Set 2: 10-12	———	1
Seated Row	Set 3: 8-10	———	1
Reverse Grip Pull Down	Set 4: 6-8	———	1
Dumbbell Row	Set 5: 20	———	0

Band/Desk Row
Two Arm Dumbbell Row
Other_____

CORE ABS
Flat Crunch
Twist Floor Crunch
Incline Crunch
Leg Raise
Twisting Ball Crunch
Ball Rollouts
Other_____

                  —————   0.5

BICEPS- ARMS (S)

Exercise	Set	Lbs.	Rest
Dumbbell Curl	Set 1: 13-15	———	1
Barbell Curls	Set 2: 10-12	———	1
Barbell Preacher Curls	Set 3: 8-10	———	1
Dumbbell Hammer Curl	Set 4: 6-8	———	1
Dumbbell/Ball Seated Curl	Set 5: 20	———	0

Dumbbell/Ball Preacher Curl
Other_____

Workout 1

Always: Warm-up with an eight- ten minute light cardiovascular exercise of choice, then start with a warm-up set using fifty percent of what you will be lifting on your first set and also stretch between sets. Fill in the chart below by selecting an exercise from each muscle group and filling in the pounds you lifted for each repetition.

(Choose one)

Exercises	Reps	Lbs.	Rest (Min.)
THIGHS (P)			
Leg Press	Set 1: 13-15	_____	1
Squats	Set 2: 10-12	_____	1
Leg Extensions	Set 3: 8-10	_____	1
Stationary Lunge	Set 4: 6-8	_____	1
Step Ups	Set 5: 20	_____	0
Ball Squat			
Other_____			
CORE ABS			
Flat Crunch	_____		0.5
Twist Floor Crunch			
Incline Crunch			
Leg Raise			
Twisting Ball Crunch			
Ball Rollouts			
Other_____			
CHEST (P)			
Flat Bench Press	Set 1: 13-15	_____	1
Incline Bench Press	Set 2: 10-12	_____	1
Machine Press	Set 3: 8-10	_____	1
Dumbbell Fly	Set 4: 6-8	_____	1
Push Ups	Set 5: 20	_____	0
Dumbbell/Ball Press			
Dumbbell/Ball Fly			
Other_____			

Page 1

140

Workout 1

(Choose one)

Exercises	Reps	Lbs.	Rest (Min.)
CORE ABS			
Flat Crunch	_____		0.5
Twist Floor Crunch			
Incline Crunch			
Leg Raise			
Twisting Ball Crunch			
Ball Rollouts			
Other_____			
SHOULDERS (S)			
Dumbbell Press	Set 1: 13-15	_____	1
Machine Press	Set 2: 10-12	_____	1
Dumbbell Side Raise	Set 3: 8-10	_____	1
Dumbbell Rear Squeeze	Set 4: 6-8	_____	1
Dumbbell/Ball Press	Set 5: 20	_____	0
Band Side Raise			
Other_____			
CORE ABS			
Flat Crunch	_____		0.5
Twist Floor Crunch			
Incline Crunch			
Leg Raise			
Twisting Ball Crunch			
Ball Rollouts			
Other_____			
TRICEPS- ARMS (S)			
Tricep Pushdown	Set 1: 13-15	_____	1
French Curls	Set 2: 10-12	_____	1
Rope Pushdowns	Set 3: 8-10	_____	1
One Arm Pushdowns	Set 4: 6-8	_____	1
Chair Dips	Set 5: 20	_____	0
Dumbbell/Ball Kickbacks			
Other_____			

Page 2

141

Workout 2

Always: Warm-up with an eight- ten minute light cardiovascular exercise of choice, then start with a warm-up set using fifty percent of what you will be lifting on your first set and also stretch between sets. Fill in the chart below by selecting an exercise from each muscle group and filling in the pounds you lifted for each repetition.

(Choose one)

Exercises	Reps	Lbs.	Rest (Min.)
BACK OF THIGH (P)			
Laying Leg Curls	Set 1: 13-15	_____	1
Dumbbell Dead Lifts	Set 2: 10-12	_____	1
Reverse Lunge	Set 3: 8-10	_____	1
Stationary Lunge	Set 4: 6-8	_____	1
Ball Curls	Set 5: 20	_____	0
Dumbbell Leg Curls			
Other_____			
CORE ABS			
Flat Crunch	_____		0.5
Twist Floor Crunch			
Incline Crunch			
Leg Raise			
Twisting Ball Crunch			
Ball Rollouts			
Other_____			
CALVES (P)			
Standing Raise	Set 1: 13-15	_____	1
Seated Raise	Set 2: 10-12	_____	1
Leg Press	Set 3: 8-10	_____	1
One Leg Raise	Set 4: 6-8	_____	1
Two Leg Dumbbell Raise	Set 5: 20	_____	0
Other_____			

Page 1

142

Workout 2

(Choose one)

Exercises	Reps	Lbs.	Rest (Min.)
CORE ABS			
Flat Crunch	_____		0.5
Twist Floor Crunch			
Incline Crunch			
Leg Raise			
Twisting Ball Crunch			
Ball Rollouts			
Other_____			

BACK (P)			
Straight Bar Pull Down	Set 1: 13-15	_____	1
Close Grip Pull	Set 2: 10-12	_____	1
Seated Row	Set 3: 8-10	_____	1
Reverse Grip Pull Down	Set 4: 6-8	_____	1
Dumbbell Row	Set 5: 20	_____	0
Band/Desk Row			
Two Arm Dumbbell Row			
Other_____			

CORE ABS			
Flat Crunch	_____		0.5
Twist Floor Crunch			
Incline Crunch			
Leg Raise			
Twisting Ball Crunch			
Ball Rollouts			
Other_____			

BICEPS- ARMS (S)			
Dumbbell Curl	Set 1: 13-15	_____	1
Barbell Curls	Set 2: 10-12	_____	1
Barbell Preacher Curls	Set 3: 8-10	_____	1
Dumbbell Hammer Curl	Set 4: 6-8	_____	1
Dumbbell/Ball Seated Curl	Set 5: 20	_____	0
Dumbbell/Ball Preacher Curl			
Other_____			

Page 2

143

Cardio

Cardiovascular Exercise
Do your cardio three to five times a week.
(Choose one)
Bike; Bleachers; Elliptical; Sprints; Track; Treadmill; Other
Time / Duration:
MPH (speed):
Level:
Target Heart Rate:
 # Of Bleachers / Sprints:

Cardiovascular Exercise
Do your cardio three to five times a week.
(Choose one)
Bike; Bleachers; Elliptical; Sprints; Track; Treadmill; Other
Time / Duration:
MPH (speed):
Level:
Target Heart Rate:
 # Of Bleachers / Sprints:

Cardiovascular Exercise
Do your cardio three to five times a week.
(Choose one)
Bike; Bleachers; Elliptical; Sprints; Track; Treadmill; Other
Time / Duration:
MPH (speed):
Level:
Target Heart Rate:
 # Of Bleachers / Sprints:

Cardio

Cardiovascular Exercise
Do your cardio three to five times a week.
(Choose one)
Bike; Bleachers; Elliptical; Sprints; Track; Treadmill; Other
Time / Duration:
MPH (speed):
Level:
Target Heart Rate:
 # Of Bleachers / Sprints:

Cardiovascular Exercise
Do your cardio three to five times a week.
(Choose one)
Bike; Bleachers; Elliptical; Sprints; Track; Treadmill; Other
Time / Duration:
MPH (speed):
Level:
Target Heart Rate:
 # Of Bleachers / Sprints:

Chapter Seven

Suffering

"Know Pain...Know Gain"

Mark J Geiger

The title of this chapter was inspired by a client of mine who was complaining about an exercise that she hates to do. Before I could even say something positive to overcome the negativity of her statement she quickly said, "I know, no pain, no gain, right?" Little did she know how right she was and little did she know that not only was what she said true for us physically, but that her statement was filled with abundant spiritual wisdom. You see it is difficult to experience spiritual growth and maturity in the absence of pain and suffering.

As I look back over the times in my life when I have matured the most, learned the most, and grown the most, it was all during the times when I hurt the most. My experiences of pain and growth, occurring simultaneously, are not unique as I am sure everyone can empathize with what I am describing. In fact, Peter not only confirms this truth for us but also comforts us as he writes, *Dear friends, do not be surprised at the painful trial you are suffering, as though something strange were happening to you. But rejoice that you participate in the sufferings of Christ, so that you may be overjoyed when his glory is revealed.* (1 Peter 4:12-13)

We live in isolation and great vanity when we believe that our pain and suffering is strange or unwarranted. When we falsely believe that we should be free from pain and suffering we deny the truth that it is God's plan for us to be healed and reconciled to Him in a holy and unconditional loving relationship through our identification with the suffering of Christ. God's plan, which clearly includes suffering is presented in the Hebrew Testament when Isaiah writes, *But He was pierced for our transgressions, He was crushed for our iniquities; the punishment that brought us peace was upon Him, and by His wounds we are healed.* (Isaiah 53:5)

If God was willing to suffer to give us a reconciliatory peace shouldn't we be able to suffer a little for Him? And furthermore, I believe God is still suffering with us today.

The movie Field of Dreams is one of my favorite movies of all time. You remember that Field of Dreams was a movie about baseball, fulfilling dreams, and a son's need to have closure on his relationship with his deceased father. The movie carried an incredible spiritual undertone that challenged each of us to reflect on our relationship with our Father in Heaven. In the movie, Costner kept hearing the voice whisper to him… "Ease His Pain". As I meditated on that I came to the conclusion that there is a universal pain that everyone must feel by default as being a part of the human race. Furthermore, through divine revelation, it occurred to me that we are not alone in our pain and that God still feels every ounce of it with us. We see the evidence of His pain in Genesis. *The Lord saw how great man's wickedness on the earth had become, and that every inclination of the thoughts of his heart was only evil all the time. The Lord was grieved that he had made man on the earth, and his heart was filled with* **pain.** (Genesis 6:5-6)

Yes, God feels our pain too! Again, in the movie, the small still voice was continually telling Ray (Costner), to ease his father's pain. In Ray's rebellious youth he held his father personally responsible for the pain that he felt after the death of his mother. He stopped playing baseball, he went to the furthest college away from home, and he did everything opposite of his father that he could just to spite him. Ray was blaming his father for all of his pain. How many of us are blaming other people for our pain? How many of us are unforgiving of our family members, ex-spouses, or ex-business partners for the pain that occurred in our relationships with them from 5, 10, even 25 years ago? Or worse yet, how many of us are blaming God for our pain? Scriptures are very clear about where pain originated and still originates from. Pain and or separation from God are a direct result of sin (free-will). We first experienced pain as a result of the original sin as it is documented in the third chapter of Genesis. *To Adam he said, "Because you listened to your wife and ate from the tree about which I commanded you, `You must not eat of it,' "Cursed is the ground because of you; through* _painful_ *toil you will eat of it all the days of your life.* (Genesis 3:17)

We see that this curse would endure without cure from their generation to ours with another example from the Hebrew Testament in Jeremiah. We also see in the latter part of this same scripture, that God promises restoration and healing.

Why do you cry out over your wound, your pain that has no cure? Because of your great guilt and many sins I have done these things to you...17But I will restore you to health and heal your wounds,' declares the Lord, (Jeremiah 30:15&17)

The acceptance of pain, the acknowledgment that it comes from our own sins and our own choices, and the declaration of your personal responsibility (accountability) of it before God is the only way to be completely and eternally restored both physically and spiritually. There is no other way. Regardless of your religious doctrine, within the universal Christian Church, we all have the common ground of the Lord's prayer to go by in which the Lord teaches us to pray, "forgive us our sins as we forgive those who sin against us." The Lord goes on to say *"For if you forgive men when they sin against you, your heavenly Father will also forgive you. But if you do not forgive men their sins, your Father will not forgive your sins."*

That is one way that we can ease our pain. We can give forgiveness and seek it for ourselves. We further discuss the importance of forgiveness on your physical health in a later chapter but for now you need to know that God will meet you wherever your pain/suffering is at. If it is at the point of addiction, He will meet you. If it is at the point of unfaithfulness, He will meet you. If it is at the point of sexual immorality, He will meet you. If it is at the point of greed, He will meet you. All you have to do is cry to the Lord with the same sincerity of David as he cried out...*I am in pain and distress; may your salvation, O God, protect me.* (Psalm 69:29) I guess we could even say that if we *"Ease His pain"*, we will ease our own pain. But not always, and especially not on a physical level!

Our suffering as I mentioned earlier can often be for our own good. Physical exercise is a great example that illustrates this spiritual principle. If we are willing to suffer through the uncomfortable burning sensations in our muscles, or the lactic acid build up that causes stiffness, or the shortness of breath and increase of body temperatures during exercise; then we can yield the healthy benefits that result from the discomfort. Remember, the physical is a reflection of the spiritual.

I know this is a difficult concept for us to comprehend with our limited human intellect, especially when we are repeatedly taught that God is a God of love and compassion. But the fact of the matter is though; our ever present free will in this world is ironically conditional on our pre-destined bondage to sin. If we were without sin, we would be without suffering, and there would be no need for God, or His son as our Savior. Our ability to choose moment by moment, circumstance by circumstance; to choose joy in the midst of suffering, to choose repentance in the face of sin, and to choose to put our Faith in an eternal spiritual life when we are ever so aware of the absolution of our physical death, is exactly what connects us to our Father, our creator...our advocate.

So now I ask each of you a personal and difficult question. What pains are you faced with this very moment? Are you faced with unemployment? Are you faced with the possibility of a failed marriage or another broken relationship? Are you faced with the truth that your child is a drug addict? Are you faced with the truth that you have spent a lifetime pursuing money, relationships, and things that have brought you only temporary satisfaction and now your health is in disarray? While evil and sin may or may not be at the root of the things causing your current pain, take heart because **"this"** is exactly what God knew would bring you closer to Him. *To this you were called, because Christ suffered for you, leaving you an example that you should follow in his steps.* (1 Peter 2:21)

Maybe your current problem is not any of the drastic pains listed above. Maybe yours is simply a weight problem. Have you ever thought your weight problem could bring you closer to God? It can because whatever "this" may happen to be for you at this given moment in your life, it is exactly what God wants to use to bring you in closer communion with Him. You can choose to deal with it on your own in self pity, or you can find peace and joy as you seek God during your deliverance of "this" suffering.

Look at the lady who touched the hem of Jesus garment. You remember the story...*And a woman was there who had been subject to bleeding for twelve years. She had suffered a great deal under the care of many doctors and had spent all she had, yet instead of getting better she grew worse. When she heard about Jesus, she came up behind him in the crowd and touched his cloak, because she thought, "If I just touch his clothes, I will be healed." Immediately her bleeding stopped and she felt in her body that she was freed from her suffering.* (Mark 5:25-29)

This woman had been suffering for *twelve* years! She spent all of her money on cures to no avail. How many of us have spent all of our money on vitamins, supplements, health club memberships and cheesy infomercial products to no avail? Perhaps it is because we have not embraced the truth about suffering.

Suffering comes in many forms. In reminding you about covenants, sometimes we have to suffer to keep our word. King David, a warrior King and business man, knew the meaning of suffering to keep a covenant. In Psalm 15 David asks the Lord two questions; who can dwell with Him and who can live with Him on His holy hill? Among the numerous answers to these two questions we find in verse 4, the answer to who can live with the Lord is he *"who keeps his oath even when it hurts."*

That's what I am talking about people! Pain is good for us from time to time. Pain puts us in touch with reality and is a feeling that not only humbles us, but also causes us to reflect on our choices, attitudes and behavior. I love doing the right thing even when it hurts or costs me something because I know that God is watching and will be pleased with my suffering.

Call me crazy but I love the stiffness in my legs that almost keeps me from walking down a flight of stairs even two and three days after my last workout. It is that discomfort, that pain; that welcome suffering that lets me know I am alive and that both God and I can be pleased with my physical walk before Him.

God knows that we are only physical beings in the absence of His Holy Spirit, and like Him, I too realize that we do not like to suffer nor do we even like to talk about suffering. So if this chapter was a buzz kill for some of you who don't like being stretched either physically or spiritually beyond your comfort zone then take heart as I remind you of an awesome promise, one you can look forward to, one more pleasurable than your next vacation, your next shopping spree, or your next relationship. The promise is this. In the end all of your pain and suffering will be gone as it is written...

And I heard a loud voice from the throne saying, "Now the dwelling of God is with men, and he will live with them. They will be his people, and God himself will be with them and be their God. He will wipe every tear from their eyes. There will be no more death or mourning or crying or pain, for the old order of things has passed away." (Revelation 21:3-4)

Chapter/Week Seven
Spiritual Workout

1. What was the greatest time of suffering that you have ever experienced in your life and how did you endure it?

_____

_____

_____

_____

_____

_____

_____

2. How did Jesus suffering benefit us? Did your suffering listed above have any benefit to it? Did it draw you closer to God? How?

_____

_____

_____

_____

_____

_____

_____

_____

_____

3. Why do we have to suffer?

_____

_____

_____

_____

_____

_____

_____

_____

_____

4. Describe how you have embraced any physical discomfort from your exercise workouts and how it has helped you to become healthier?

_____

_____

_____

_____

_____

_____

_____

_____

5. What scripture can you write down below and recall when you need help getting through any suffering you may experience?

_____

_____

_____

_____

_____

_____

_____

_____

Workout 1

Always: Warm-up with an eight- ten minute light cardiovascular exercise of choice, then start with a warm-up set using fifty percent of what you will be lifting on your first set and also stretch between sets. Fill in the chart below by selecting an exercise from each muscle group and filling in the pounds you lifted for each repetition.

(Choose one)

Exercises	Reps	Lbs.	Rest (Min.)
THIGHS (P)			
Leg Press	Set 1: 13-15	_____	1
Squats	Set 2: 10-12	_____	1
Leg Extensions	Set 3: 8-10	_____	1
Stationary Lunge	Set 4: 6-8	_____	1
Step Ups	Set 5: 20	_____	0
Ball Squat			
Other_____			
CORE ABS			
Flat Crunch		_____	0.5
Twist Floor Crunch			
Incline Crunch			
Leg Raise			
Twisting Ball Crunch			
Ball Rollouts			
Other_____			
CHEST (P)			
Flat Bench Press	Set 1: 13-15	_____	1
Incline Bench Press	Set 2: 10-12	_____	1
Machine Press	Set 3: 8-10	_____	1
Dumbbell Fly	Set 4: 6-8	_____	1
Push Ups	Set 5: 20	_____	0
Dumbbell/Ball Press			
Dumbbell/Ball Fly			
Other_____			

Page 1

156

Workout 1

(Choose one)

Exercises	Reps	Lbs.	Rest (Min.)
CORE ABS			
Flat Crunch	___		0.5
Twist Floor Crunch			
Incline Crunch			
Leg Raise			
Twisting Ball Crunch			
Ball Rollouts			
Other_____			

SHOULDERS (S)			
Dumbbell Press	Set 1: 13-15	___	1
Machine Press	Set 2: 10-12	___	1
Dumbbell Side Raise	Set 3: 8-10	___	1
Dumbbell Rear Squeeze	Set 4: 6-8	___	1
Dumbbell/Ball Press	Set 5: 20	___	0
Band Side Raise			
Other_____			

CORE ABS			
Flat Crunch	___		0.5
Twist Floor Crunch			
Incline Crunch			
Leg Raise			
Twisting Ball Crunch			
Ball Rollouts			
Other_____			

TRICEPS- ARMS (S)			
Tricep Pushdown	Set 1: 13-15	___	1
French Curls	Set 2: 10-12	___	1
Rope Pushdowns	Set 3: 8-10	___	1
One Arm Pushdowns	Set 4: 6-8	___	1
Chair Dips	Set 5: 20	___	0
Dumbbell/Ball Kickbacks			
Other_____			

Page 2

157

Workout 2

Always: Warm-up with an eight- ten minute light cardiovascular exercise of choice, then start with a warm-up set using fifty percent of what you will be lifting on your first set and also stretch between sets. Fill in the chart below by selecting an exercise from each muscle group and filling in the pounds you lifted for each repetition.

(Choose one)

Exercises	Reps	Lbs.	Rest (Min.)
BACK OF THIGH (P)			
Laying Leg Curls	Set 1: 13-15	_____	1
Dumbbell Dead Lifts	Set 2: 10-12	_____	1
Reverse Lunge	Set 3: 8-10	_____	1
Stationary Lunge	Set 4: 6-8	_____	1
Ball Curls	Set 5: 20	_____	0
Dumbbell Leg Curls			
Other_____			
CORE ABS			
Flat Crunch		_____	0.5
Twist Floor Crunch			
Incline Crunch			
Leg Raise			
Twisting Ball Crunch			
Ball Rollouts			
Other_____			
CALVES (P)			
Standing Raise	Set 1: 13-15	_____	1
Seated Raise	Set 2: 10-12	_____	1
Leg Press	Set 3: 8-10	_____	1
One Leg Raise	Set 4: 6-8	_____	1
Two Leg Dumbbell Raise	Set 5: 20	_____	0
Other_____			

Page 1

158

Workout 2

(Choose one)

Exercises	Reps	Lbs.	Rest (Min.)
CORE ABS			
Flat Crunch	_____		0.5
Twist Floor Crunch			
Incline Crunch			
Leg Raise			
Twisting Ball Crunch			
Ball Rollouts			
Other_____			

BACK (P)			
Straight Bar Pull Down	Set 1: 13-15	_____	1
Close Grip Pull	Set 2: 10-12	_____	1
Seated Row	Set 3: 8-10	_____	1
Reverse Grip Pull Down	Set 4: 6-8	_____	1
Dumbbell Row	Set 5: 20	_____	0
Band/Desk Row			
Two Arm Dumbbell Row			
Other_____			

CORE ABS			
Flat Crunch	_____		0.5
Twist Floor Crunch			
Incline Crunch			
Leg Raise			
Twisting Ball Crunch			
Ball Rollouts			
Other_____			

BICEPS- ARMS (S)			
Dumbbell Curl	Set 1: 13-15	_____	1
Barbell Curls	Set 2: 10-12	_____	1
Barbell Preacher Curls	Set 3: 8-10	_____	1
Dumbbell Hammer Curl	Set 4: 6-8	_____	1
Dumbbell/Ball Seated Curl	Set 5: 20	_____	0
Dumbbell/Ball Preacher Curl			
Other_____			

Page 2

159

Workout 1

Always: Warm-up with an eight- ten minute light cardiovascular exercise of choice, then start with a warm-up set using fifty percent of what you will be lifting on your first set and also stretch between sets. Fill in the chart below by selecting an exercise from each muscle group and filling in the pounds you lifted for each repetition.

(Choose one)

Exercises	Reps	Lbs.	Rest (Min.)
THIGHS (P)			
Leg Press	Set 1: 13-15	_____	1
Squats	Set 2: 10-12	_____	1
Leg Extensions	Set 3: 8-10	_____	1
Stationary Lunge	Set 4: 6-8	_____	1
Step Ups	Set 5: 20	_____	0
Ball Squat			
Other_____			
CORE ABS			
Flat Crunch		_____	0.5
Twist Floor Crunch			
Incline Crunch			
Leg Raise			
Twisting Ball Crunch			
Ball Rollouts			
Other_____			
CHEST (P)			
Flat Bench Press	Set 1: 13-15	_____	1
Incline Bench Press	Set 2: 10-12	_____	1
Machine Press	Set 3: 8-10	_____	1
Dumbbell Fly	Set 4: 6-8	_____	1
Push Ups	Set 5: 20	_____	0
Dumbbell/Ball Press			
Dumbbell/Ball Fly			
Other_____			

Page 1

Workout 1

(Choose one)

Exercises	Reps	Lbs.	Rest (Min.)
CORE ABS			
Flat Crunch	_____		0.5
Twist Floor Crunch			
Incline Crunch			
Leg Raise			
Twisting Ball Crunch			
Ball Rollouts			
Other _____			

Exercises	Reps	Lbs.	Rest (Min.)
SHOULDERS (S)			
Dumbbell Press	Set 1: 13-15	_____	1
Machine Press	Set 2: 10-12	_____	1
Dumbbell Side Raise	Set 3: 8-10	_____	1
Dumbbell Rear Squeeze	Set 4: 6-8	_____	1
Dumbbell/Ball Press	Set 5: 20	_____	0
Band Side Raise			
Other _____			

Exercises	Reps	Lbs.	Rest (Min.)
CORE ABS			
Flat Crunch	_____		0.5
Twist Floor Crunch			
Incline Crunch			
Leg Raise			
Twisting Ball Crunch			
Ball Rollouts			
Other _____			

Exercises	Reps	Lbs.	Rest (Min.)
TRICEPS- ARMS (S)			
Tricep Pushdown	Set 1: 13-15	_____	1
French Curls	Set 2: 10-12	_____	1
Rope Pushdowns	Set 3: 8-10	_____	1
One Arm Pushdowns	Set 4: 6-8	_____	1
Chair Dips	Set 5: 20	_____	0
Dumbbell/Ball Kickbacks			
Other _____			

Cardio

Cardiovascular Exercise
Do your cardio three to five times a week.
(Choose one)
Bike; Bleachers; Elliptical; Sprints; Track; Treadmill; Other
Time / Duration:
MPH (speed):
Level:
Target Heart Rate:
 # Of Bleachers / Sprints:

Cardiovascular Exercise
Do your cardio three to five times a week.
(Choose one)
Bike; Bleachers; Elliptical; Sprints; Track; Treadmill; Other
Time / Duration:
MPH (speed):
Level:
Target Heart Rate:
 # Of Bleachers / Sprints:

Cardiovascular Exercise
Do your cardio three to five times a week.
(Choose one)
Bike; Bleachers; Elliptical; Sprints; Track; Treadmill; Other
Time / Duration:
MPH (speed):
Level:
Target Heart Rate:
 # Of Bleachers / Sprints:

Cardio

Cardiovascular Exercise

Do your cardio three to five times a week.
(Choose one)
Bike; Bleachers; Elliptical; Sprints; Track; Treadmill; Other
Time / Duration:
MPH (speed):
Level:
Target Heart Rate:
 # Of Bleachers / Sprints:

Cardiovascular Exercise

Do your cardio three to five times a week.
(Choose one)
Bike; Bleachers; Elliptical; Sprints; Track; Treadmill; Other
Time / Duration:
MPH (speed):
Level:
Target Heart Rate:
 # Of Bleachers / Sprints:

Page 2

163

Chapter Eight

Attitude

"It's not your aptitude that sets your altitude...it's your attitude."

Pastor Ed Young

Let me tell you right now this is the longest chapter in the book. That should tell you that your attitude is the most important component on your physical walk with God. The sum of your attitude is comprised of a sound mind, thankfulness over bitterness, joy over sorrow, courage over fear and proper motivation

The Attitude of a <u>Sound Mind</u>

The movie *A Beautiful Mind* was a deeply moving human drama about a true genius, inspired by happenings in the life of mathematician John Forbes Nash, Jr. The handsome and highly eccentric Nash made an astounding discovery early in life and stood on the threshold of international acclaim. But his quick ascent into the intellectual stratosphere radically changed course when Nash's intuitive brilliance was undermined by schizophrenia. Facing challenges that have destroyed many others, Nash fought back, with the help of his devoted wife Alicia. After decades of hardship, he triumphed over tragedy, and received the Nobel Prize in 1994. A living legend, Nash continues to pursue his work today.

Each of us is like Nash in a way in the sense that we all also have beautiful minds. And while we may not have to overcome schizophrenia in order for our minds to flourish and our glory to be revealed, we do need to pay close attention to our thoughts, the voices we hear, and the images that we see. The term schizophrenia includes a group of psychotic disorders usually characterized by withdrawal from reality, illogical patterns of thinking, delusions, and hallucinations. In the world we live in, it doesn't matter that we don't suffer from uncontrollable hallucinations because with an ever increasing liberal media and the World Wide Web we are often bombarded with less than beautiful images that affect our minds with subtle and blatant negativity.

And while we don't have to worry about any involuntary withdrawals from reality, we still have to worry about being involuntarily drawn into the delusions of television programming that is in fact far from reality and plaguing our living rooms. For Christians the mind is a crucial element of our bodies that we need to pay constant attention to for the purposes of achieving and maintaining good spiritual and physical health. Everyone knows the following scripture, Jesus replied: *"Love the Lord your God with all your heart and with all your soul and with all your _mind_.'* (Matthew 22:37)

With that said we need to know how to love the Lord with our mind. We need to know how to train our minds. I spent five years in college learning how to train the body and unfortunately was not ever taught how to train the mind. I am sure many of you went to school to learn your professional trades as well but were not ever taught about how to control your thoughts. As adults we need to learn, if we have not already, how to discern our thoughts from being the truth or lies, from being harmful or helpful, from being pure or impure. If our minds are not processing our life circumstances correctly we are in jeopardy of developing heart problems. Now when I say heart problems I am not talking just about clogged arteries, I am talking about anger, bitterness, jealousy, resentment, greed, and lust because it is out of our broken and confused hearts that all these things come. So, with the revelation that the world is in fact assaulting our minds daily we can truly understand the significance of what Paul writes in Romans when he says, *Do not conform any longer to the pattern of this world, but be transformed by the renewing of your mind.* (Romans 12:2)

Okay, that sounds great. Lets transform and renew our minds because deep down, and even though we may not talk about it at the family reunions, we know that if we could just stop overeating...if we could just stop smoking or drinking...if we could just stop looking at pornography on the Internet...if we could just stop spending more money than we make on things that we don't need...if we could just stop seeking our self worth from the way our bodies look...if we could just stopping seeking approval and acceptance from people for the things we accomplish at work; we would have that peace that we so desperately need.

We all have problems, some more severe than others but nonetheless we all have them. Our problems all start externally, then we process them through our *minds* internally, and finally we manifest the results of our thoughts externally again through our speech and our behavior.

So then what do we do? This is what we do, *Finally, brothers, whatever is true, whatever is noble, whatever is right, whatever is pure, whatever is lovely, whatever is admirable–if anything is excellent or praiseworthy–think about such things.* (Philippians 4:7-8)

Okay great, just have pure thoughts and your mind will be renewed. This sounds easy right? Its not and there is a reason why it is not. The reason goes far beyond you and me. It is one of epic proportion. The fall of man, our peace and rest in God, our eternal residence in the Garden of Eden was tragically and catastrophically stolen from each of us prior to our existence. It was stolen as a result of an assault on Eve's mind and it is no different for us today. *"But I am afraid that just as Eve was deceived by the serpent's cunning, your minds may somehow be led astray from your sincere and pure devotion to Christ."* (2 Corinthians 11:3)

And why are we not aware of these assaults? Why is it that not everyone can see and hear in the spiritual realm? Why is it that not everyone believes in or is aware of the sinister beings that stalk our minds, hearts and souls? Why is it that not everyone who reads the bible can understand the words that are written in it? It is because… *"The god of this age (satan) has blinded the minds of unbelievers, so that they cannot see the light of the gospel of the glory of Christ, who is the image of God."* (2 Corinthians 4:3-6)

You see, most of us have been blinded and we will remain blinded until we call out to God **by faith** asking Him to show us the truth, asking Him to open our minds to spiritual discernment.

So back to the movie *A Beautiful Mind* where I started with this. How did Nash overcome his challenges and hardships? He did it using the same mind that was diseased with schizophrenia. He did it with the help of loved ones (support). He was constantly on guard. My favorite part of the whole movie was in the end when he turned to his student in the hallway and asked if the guy that was standing there talking to him was real or not. If Nash could over come what he did to show the world the beautiful sound mind that God gave him, then you and I can do the same. And we must do the same if we are going to be spiritually and physically healthy. The following are a few scriptures that will help us maintain a sound mind and the right attitude. Feed on these daily.

Therefore, prepare your <u>minds</u> for action; be self-controlled; set your hope fully on the grace to be given you when Jesus Christ is revealed. As obedient children, do not conform to the evil desires you had when you lived in ignorance. But just as he who called you is holy, so be holy in all you do; for it is written: "Be holy, because I am holy." (1 Peter 1:13-16)

Once you were alienated from God and were enemies in your <u>minds</u> because of your evil behavior. But now he has reconciled you by Christ's physical body through death to present you holy in his sight, without blemish and free from accusation— (Colossians 1:21-22)

Those who live according to the sinful nature have their <u>minds</u> set on what that nature desires; but those who live in accordance with the Spirit have their <u>minds</u> set on what the Spirit desires. The <u>mind</u> of sinful man is death, but the <u>mind</u> controlled by the Spirit is life and peace; the sinful <u>mind</u> is hostile to God. It does not submit to God's law, nor can it do so. Those controlled by the sinful nature cannot please God. (Romans 8:5-8)

You were taught, with regard to your former way of life, to put off your old self, which is being corrupted by its deceitful desires; to be made new in the attitude of your <u>minds</u>; and to put on the new self, created to be like God in true righteousness and holiness. (Ephesians 4:22-2)

Set your <u>minds</u> on things above, not on earthly things. (Colossians 3:2)

The Attitude of <u>Thanksgiving</u>

Most of us celebrate thanksgiving as a single November holiday when in reality we should be celebrating it as a lifestyle.

You see I have learned that expressing gratitude on a daily basis is one of those emotions that lead to great health. The fact is, a series of studies have shown that gratitude not only promotes physical and emotional well-being, but also improves one's ability to cope with stress and strengthens positive interaction with others. Furthermore, research shows grateful individuals report having more energy and less physical complaints than those who don't express this emotion! Health professionals and the medical community have known for years that healthy emotions even enhance heart health by interrupting the hormonal stress responses caused by negative emotions. So with the verdict in, what can you and I do on a daily basis to improve our thankfulness and health simultaneously?

There are two fairly simple things we can do. We can:

Set aside at least 5 or 10 minutes per day to meditate and pray about the things that we're most thankful for.

We can also write these things down in a notebook or journal. Writing further enhances the effectiveness of this time because we have to engage the mind in the process of thinking about what we are going to write. It also engages our senses on a higher level when we visually see what we are thankful for.

As far as the time of day to do this, for most people it should be done whenever they can fit it into their hectic schedules. However, ideally it is better to do it first thing in the morning or last thing at night before falling asleep. A thankful attitude in the morning sets the tone for the day and positions you to handle any stress coming your way later on. On the other hand, a thankful attitude in the evening allows you to let go of all the stress that you accumulated throughout the day and allows you to have healthier and more productive sleep cycles. I tend to do it two times a day myself, both a.m. and p.m.

But regardless of the time of day that you end up choosing, be sure to commit to doing it on a regular basis and don't allow anything to prevent it. It's the *habit* of expressing the emotion of thankfulness that leads to the accumulation of the benefits.

Another way to incorporate a thankful attitude into our life is by giving thanks at every meal. Look at the example of thanksgiving that Christ gave us when He fed the 5000. *"Bring them here to me," he said. And he directed the people to sit down on the grass. Taking the five loaves and the two fish and looking up to heaven, **he gave thanks** and broke the loaves. Then he gave them to the disciples, and the disciples gave them to the people.* (Matthew 14:18-19)

He did the same thing a chapter later with 4000 more people. *He told the crowd to sit down on the ground. Then he took the seven loaves and the fish, **and when he had given thanks,** he broke them and gave them to the disciples, and they in turn to the people.*(Matthew15:35-36)

And what about at the last supper? He didn't just give thanks once, but He did it twice in the same meal! *While they were eating,*

*Jesus took bread, **gave thanks** and broke it, and gave it to his disciples, saying, "Take and eat; this is my body." Then he took the cup, **gave thanks** and offered it to them, saying, "Drink from it, all of you. This is my blood of the covenant, which is poured out for many for the forgiveness of sins.* (Matthew 26:26-28)

The bottom line is Jesus was thankful and that means that we need to be thankful...at all times about all things and our thanks should be directed to God. In Paul's preaching to the Ephesians he said, *Sing and make music in your heart to the Lord, always giving thanks to God the Father for everything, in the name of our Lord Jesus Christ.*(5:19-20)

Bottom line...a thankful attitude leads to better physical and spiritual health.

The Attitude of Joy

Although being joyful is different than being happy the following song lyrics seem appropriate for this section.

Don't Worry, Be Happy

Here's a little song I wrote
You might want to sing it note for note
Don't worry, be happy.
In every life we have some trouble
But when you worry you make it double
Don't worry, be happy.
Don't worry, be happy now.

Ain't got no place to lay your head
Somebody came and took your bed
Don't worry, be happy.
The landlord say your rent is late
He may have to litigate
Don't worry, be happy.

CHORUS: (Look at me – I'm happy. Don't worry, be happy.
Here I give you my phone number. When you worry, call me,
I make you happy. Don't worry, be happy.)

Ain't got no cash, ain't got no style
Ain't got no gal to make you smile
Don't worry, be happy.
'Cause when you worry your face will frown
And that will bring everybody down
Don't worry, be happy.

CHORUS: (Don't worry, don't worry, don't do it.
Be happy. Put a smile on your face.
Don't bring everybody down.
Don't worry. **It will soon pass, whatever it is.**
Don't worry, be happy.
I'm not worried, I'm happy...)

Bobby McFerrin

You remember that song. It was silly and fun but it exemplifies
the joyful attitude we should each have. Joy marks the fruit of
the Holy Spirit at work in our lives. *But the fruit of the Spirit is love,*
joy, peace, patience, kindness, goodness, faithfulness, gentleness and self-
control... (Galatians 5:22-23)

In addition to being a fruit of the spirit, joy is always associated
with Jesus Christ. In the New Testament joy is always found in
connection with salvation **and** *suffering*. What an odd
combination right? Wrong. If you have salvation it makes

suffering bearable. Of course nobody wants to suffer the pain of poor health or from a terminal disease or the loss of a loved one; but knowing that both you and the fellow Christians you love are going to continue on with life in a heavenly place where there is no disease, where there is no pain, where there is no death; that's the knowledge that creates joy in any circumstance you may have to face today. But to have that knowledge and experience this joy that I am speaking of you have to believe, with all certainty, that there is life after death which was made possible by the birth, death, and resurrection of Jesus Christ.

It's just like the song says, *in every life we have some trouble but when we worry we make it double*! When I look around these days I see lots of people doubling their trouble. People seem to have more worry than joy. We worry about our health, our weight, the way we look, about our jobs, our bills, or other non-sense. I have one word for anyone who is worrying. STOP! **"An anxious heart weighs a man down, but a kind word cheers him up!"** (Proverbs 25:12) Believing and living that scripture alone may help you lose weight.

If you won't take my word for it or a proverb from King Solomon, then how about what Jesus taught? He taught, *"Therefore I tell you, do not worry about your life, what you will eat or drink; or about your body, what you will wear...look at the birds of the air; they do not sow or reap or store away in barns, and yet our heavenly Father feeds them. Are you not much more valuable than they?* (Matthew 6:25)

Worry not only goes against the spiritual principles just mentioned above but it also causes disease. Worry can cause physical symptoms in your body. They include anxiety, the inability to relax, tension headaches, sleeplessness, heart palpitations, feelings of tightness in the chest, belching, nausea, and diarrhea. That doesn't sound too healthy to me. Interestingly enough, studies have shown that worry can be caused by a diet high in refined foods, particularly sugar (a food in red). In addition to all of these physical drawbacks, when we are worried we don't always act with confidence and courage, which leads us to the next important part of your attitude, courage!

But before we get to courage I want you to begin thinking about that song on a regular basis. Its melody is catchy and as I said before it may seem silly but it is deeply profound. If you find yourself worrying think of the verse towards the end when he says, *"Don't worry. It will soon pass whatever it is"*.

The phrase "Gam zeh ya'avor" is a Hebrew saying that means, "This too shall pass." Whatever you are worried about…it will pass!

The Attitude of <u>Courage</u>

I'll never forget how the Lord impressed the importance of that previous scripture (Matthew 6:25) on me. I was driving down the road one day in between appointments and I was really worried and anxious about how the business was doing financially when all of the sudden I heard a loud thump. A bird had flown right across my windshield and actually hit it. Unharmed, but probably just as scared as I was, the bird flew off after God had brought the previous scripture to my mind.

To this day, I always look for the birds flying back and forth in front of my car. They seem to always show up when my mind is wandering and worrying about the unknown. It's as if God is sending us the same message everyday. This week when you are driving in your car, notice the single bird that flies past your windshield. It'll happen to you too and when it does you will remember the scripture above. You will be reminded that the birds are fed every single day, and have been for thousands of years. The more that you begin to notice God's care for the birds, you will realize that not a day has passed in your lifetime that your needs have not been met. You may not have everything you want today, but that is not apart of the deal. Remember you're on a walk, not a sprint. Jesus goes on to say in that same passage, verse 32, *For the pagans run after all these things, and your Heavenly Father knows that you need them. But seek first his kingdom and his righteousness, and all these things will be given to you as well.*

Once you overcome your worries you can exude a confidence and *courage* in your search for God knowing that you will be given everything you need.

When I think of the word courage I think of the famous Nike campaign, "Just Do It!" Everybody is familiar with Nike's just do it campaign. It was without a doubt one of the most successfully branded campaigns in fitness apparel history having lasted nearly two decades. Those three, one syllable words, while simple enough, were often supplemented with powerful images of lean bodies diligently working, profusely sweating, and relentlessly enduring intense physical strain. The Nike athletes and models always displayed courage and that is why their campaign was so successful. The commercials appealed to the human nature, the desire to overcome at all cost, even if it meant intense *suffering.*

5000 years before the Just Do It campaign was ever conceived Moses essentially came up with the same command. He essentially told the children of God to "Just Do It!" His exact words were, *"You have dwelt on this mountain long enough. Break camp and advance into the hill country of the Amorites; go to all the neighboring peoples in the Arabah, in the mountains, in the western foothills, in the Negev and along the coast, to the land of the Canaanites and to Lebanon, as far as the great river, the Euphrates. See, I have given you this land. Go in and take possession of the land that the Lord swore he would give to your fathers—to Abraham, Isaac and Jacob—and to their descendants after them.*"(Deuteronomy 1:6-8)

Having been led out of slavery from Egypt, the children of Israel, also known as the exodus generation, had spent approximately a year of solitude in the mountainous region of Horeb. It was purposefully a year of spiritual and physical training for them. It was there under Moses leadership that God began laying the foundation of their new life and developing their spiritual character. Upon completion of God's plan to mature them he commanded them to march straight to the land of Canaan and posses it. When you are done with this 12 week program you will have marched straight into your promised land.

The journey itself to the Promised Land was only 11 days; however their fear and *worry* of failure and ensuing disobedience caused them to be held *accountable* and they ended up wandering (*suffering*) in the desert for 40 years before eventually fulfilling God's purpose for their nation.

Many of us today are also like the children of Israel; slaves when it comes to our health and fitness. Over the years we have become slaves to inactivity, improper eating, as well as overeating. We have developed the mentality of a slave in that we have lived in bondage for so long that we are used to the despair of it and cannot envision life any other way. This has destroyed our confidence and stolen our courage. Sure, some of us desire a new vision, and from time to time even get a glimpse of one, only to watch it fade away like a mirage in the desert replaced by the fear of failure, or just as bad, disbelief.

As the story went on though, only two men out of the original exodus generation believed that they could go in and take the Promised Land with God's help. Those two men, Joshua and Caleb, displayed an attitude of *courage* and eventually they were blessed to enter Canaan, leading the next generation of Israelites. Sadly though, an entire generation of Israelites did not believe and therefore did not receive. They spent the rest of their lives wandering in the desert only to die there.

Don't be like them. Do not die wandering around worrying and afraid to receive God's promises for you. You have to believe (Faith) that God wants the best for you. You have to do what he prompts you to do (discipline). There will be battles (suffering). There will be times when defeat seems impending (worry). That is fine, historically that is the way God likes it. But make sure you recapture or acquire an attitude of *courage, joy* and *thanksgiving* knowing that you won't be alone and it won't be by your strength alone that you accomplish his will, but by His Spirit *(support)*. *"Not by might nor by power, but by my Spirit,' says the Lord Almighty.* (Zechariah 4:6)

An Attitude with __Proper Motivation__

Going back to the highly successful Nike campaign, while it was great for displaying an attitude of courage it did nothing to address the attitude of proper motivation. Viewers were left to believe that the number one reason why you should just do it was for the ultimate reward of personal accomplishment, personal achievement, and or a personal victory.

Years ago in an effort to further motivate people and encourage them at another level; I began trying to isolate the number one reason why people should "just do it". I asked clients, especially ones that had been training for years, why are you doing it? Some said they just wanted to maintain the results they achieved. Others said they hadn't yet met their goals and were continuing to press on toward them. Still, others just couldn't do it on their own without continual *support.*

While all of those responses given were certainly valid, I still sensed my question was unanswered and that there existed a much greater reason why we should all just be doing it.

In 1 Corinthians 10:31 Paul answered that question. *"So whether you eat or drink or whatever you do, do it all for the glory of God."* That's it! That is the correct attitude for proper motivation. Your motivation, the number one reason to *just do it,* is for the glory of God.

Over the years I witnessed many people fail to achieve their goals for a wide variety of reasons. Some lacked self-confidence (no courage) and could not overcome their past failures (*unforgiveness* and *guilt* which is addressed in Chapter 10). Others were lazy (not disciples) and just not committed (no covenant). Still others allowed external circumstances (resistance) to deter or distract them from their heart's desire. Observing their successes and failures I realized that *when our conviction or reason for doing something is anything other than for the glory of God we are left vulnerable to failure.*

While wanting to look and feel good are both natural and healthy desires, we need to tread outside of our personal reasons and commit to just doing it for God. God never fails to achieve His will and it is definitely His will for you to be blessed with great spiritual and physical health.

A final note on proper motivation we need to quickly address is the following. *Nothing in all creation is hidden from God's sight. Everything is uncovered and laid bare before the eyes of him to whom we must give account.* (Hebrews 4:13) You can fool yourself…your flesh, but you cannot fool the Holy Spirit of God dwelling in you. He knows what's in your heart. Ask Him to reveal it to you so that you can heal it and in turn have the proper motivation.

In summary of this entire chapter, a great attitude is essential in your physical and spiritual health. It encompasses and is responsible for so much more than we can possibly know. So as you train your body with physical exercises, train your mind with the spiritual principles herein feeding on the word of God that will help you become mentally sound and stable, thankful, joyful, without worry, courageous and properly motivated.

Chapter/Week Eight
Spiritual Workout

1. List the five aspects of your attitude that are important for maintaining and achieving great physical and spiritual health.

_____

_____

_____

_____

_____

_____

_____

2. In what area of your attitude do you struggle the most? Why do you think you struggle in this area?

_____

_____

_____

_____

_____

_____

_____

_____

3. Write a scripture that you will remember and one that you can recite to yourself when you have the wrong attitude.

_____

_____

_____

_____

_____

_____

_____

_____

_____

4. What scripture or occurrences in nature prove to you that God is in control and will take care of all of your needs freeing you from fear and worry?

_____

_____

_____

_____

_____

_____

_____

_____

5. What was your attitude about exercise and eating healthy prior to beginning this program? What is it like now and why?

_____

_____

_____

_____

_____

_____

_____

_____

Workout 2

Always: Warm-up with an eight- ten minute light cardiovascular exercise of choice, then start with a warm-up set using fifty percent of what you will be lifting on your first set and also stretch between sets. Fill in the chart below by selecting an exercise from each muscle group and filling in the pounds you lifted for each repetition.

(Choose one)

Exercises	Reps	Lbs.	Rest (Min.)
BACK OF THIGH (P)			
Laying Leg Curls	Set 1: 13-15	_____	1
Dumbbell Dead Lifts	Set 2: 10-12	_____	1
Reverse Lunge	Set 3: 8-10	_____	1
Stationary Lunge	Set 4: 6-8	_____	1
Ball Curls	Set 5: 20	_____	0
Dumbbell Leg Curls			
Other_____			
CORE ABS			
Flat Crunch		_____	0.5
Twist Floor Crunch			
Incline Crunch			
Leg Raise			
Twisting Ball Crunch			
Ball Rollouts			
Other_____			
CALVES (P)			
Standing Raise	Set 1: 13-15	_____	1
Seated Raise	Set 2: 10-12	_____	1
Leg Press	Set 3: 8-10	_____	1
One Leg Raise	Set 4: 6-8	_____	1
Two Leg Dumbbell Raise	Set 5: 20	_____	0
Other_____			

Page 1

184

Workout 2

(Choose one)

Exercises	Reps	Lbs.	Rest (Min.)
CORE ABS			
Flat Crunch	———		0.5
Twist Floor Crunch			
Incline Crunch			
Leg Raise			
Twisting Ball Crunch			
Ball Rollouts			
Other_____			
BACK (P)			
Straight Bar Pull Down	Set 1: 13-15	———	1
Close Grip Pull	Set 2: 10-12	———	1
Seated Row	Set 3: 8-10	———	1
Reverse Grip Pull Down	Set 4: 6-8	———	1
Dumbbell Row	Set 5: 20	———	0
Band/Desk Row			
Two Arm Dumbbell Row			
Other_____			
CORE ABS			
Flat Crunch	———		0.5
Twist Floor Crunch			
Incline Crunch			
Leg Raise			
Twisting Ball Crunch			
Ball Rollouts			
Other_____			
BICEPS- ARMS (S)			
Dumbbell Curl	Set 1: 13-15	———	1
Barbell Curls	Set 2: 10-12	———	1
Barbell Preacher Curls	Set 3: 8-10	———	1
Dumbbell Hammer Curl	Set 4: 6-8	———	1
Dumbbell/Ball Seated Curl	Set 5: 20	———	0
Dumbbell/Ball Preacher Curl			
Other_____			

Page 2

185

Workout 1

Always: Warm-up with an eight- ten minute light cardiovascular exercise of choice, then start with a warm-up set using fifty percent of what you will be lifting on your first set and also stretch between sets. Fill in the chart below by selecting an exercise from each muscle group and filling in the pounds you lifted for each repetition.

(Choose one)

Exercises	Reps	Lbs.	Rest (Min.)
THIGHS (P)			
Leg Press	Set 1: 13-15	_____	1
Squats	Set 2: 10-12	_____	1
Leg Extensions	Set 3: 8-10	_____	1
Stationary Lunge	Set 4: 6-8	_____	1
Step Ups	Set 5: 20	_____	0
Ball Squat			
Other_____			
CORE ABS			
Flat Crunch	_____		0.5
Twist Floor Crunch			
Incline Crunch			
Leg Raise			
Twisting Ball Crunch			
Ball Rollouts			
Other_____			
CHEST (P)			
Flat Bench Press	Set 1: 13-15	_____	1
Incline Bench Press	Set 2: 10-12	_____	1
Machine Press	Set 3: 8-10	_____	1
Dumbbell Fly	Set 4: 6-8	_____	1
Push Ups	Set 5: 20	_____	0
Dumbbell/Ball Press			
Dumbbell/Ball Fly			
Other_____			

Page 1

186

Workout 1

(Choose one)

Exercises	Reps	Lbs.	Rest (Min.)
CORE ABS			
Flat Crunch	_____		0.5
Twist Floor Crunch			
Incline Crunch			
Leg Raise			
Twisting Ball Crunch			
Ball Rollouts			
Other_____			
SHOULDERS (S)			
Dumbbell Press	Set 1: 13-15	_____	1
Machine Press	Set 2: 10-12	_____	1
Dumbbell Side Raise	Set 3: 8-10	_____	1
Dumbbell Rear Squeeze	Set 4: 6-8	_____	1
Dumbbell/Ball Press	Set 5: 20	_____	0
Band Side Raise			
Other_____			
CORE ABS			
Flat Crunch	_____		0.5
Twist Floor Crunch			
Incline Crunch			
Leg Raise			
Twisting Ball Crunch			
Ball Rollouts			
Other_____			
TRICEPS- ARMS (S)			
Tricep Pushdown	Set 1: 13-15	_____	1
French Curls	Set 2: 10-12	_____	1
Rope Pushdowns	Set 3: 8-10	_____	1
One Arm Pushdowns	Set 4: 6-8	_____	1
Chair Dips	Set 5: 20	_____	0
Dumbbell/Ball Kickbacks			
Other_____			

Page 2

Workout 2

Always: Warm-up with an eight- ten minute light cardiovascular exercise of choice, then start with a warm-up set using fifty percent of what you will be lifting on your first set and also stretch between sets. Fill in the chart below by selecting an exercise from each muscle group and filling in the pounds you lifted for each repetition.

(Choose one)

Exercises	Reps	Lbs.	Rest (Min.)
BACK OF THIGH (P)			
Laying Leg Curls	Set 1: 13-15	_____	1
Dumbbell Dead Lifts	Set 2: 10-12	_____	1
Reverse Lunge	Set 3: 8-10	_____	1
Stationary Lunge	Set 4: 6-8	_____	1
Ball Curls	Set 5: 20	_____	0
Dumbbell Leg Curls			
Other_____			
CORE ABS			
Flat Crunch		_____	0.5
Twist Floor Crunch			
Incline Crunch			
Leg Raise			
Twisting Ball Crunch			
Ball Rollouts			
Other_____			
CALVES (P)			
Standing Raise	Set 1: 13-15	_____	1
Seated Raise	Set 2: 10-12	_____	1
Leg Press	Set 3: 8-10	_____	1
One Leg Raise	Set 4: 6-8	_____	1
Two Leg Dumbbell Raise	Set 5: 20	_____	0
Other_____			

Page 1

Workout 2

(Choose one)

Exercises	Reps	Lbs.	Rest (Min.)

CORE ABS

Flat Crunch ——— 0.5
Twist Floor Crunch
Incline Crunch
Leg Raise
Twisting Ball Crunch
Ball Rollouts
Other_____

BACK (P)

Straight Bar Pull Down	Set 1: 13-15	———	1
Close Grip Pull	Set 2: 10-12	———	1
Seated Row	Set 3: 8-10	———	1
Reverse Grip Pull Down	Set 4: 6-8	———	1
Dumbbell Row	Set 5: 20	———	0
Band/Desk Row			
Two Arm Dumbbell Row			
Other_____			

CORE ABS

Flat Crunch ——— 0.5
Twist Floor Crunch
Incline Crunch
Leg Raise
Twisting Ball Crunch
Ball Rollouts
Other_____

BICEPS- ARMS (S)

Dumbbell Curl	Set 1: 13-15	———	1
Barbell Curls	Set 2: 10-12	———	1
Barbell Preacher Curls	Set 3: 8-10	———	1
Dumbbell Hammer Curl	Set 4: 6-8	———	1
Dumbbell/Ball Seated Curl	Set 5: 20	———	0
Dumbbell/Ball Preacher Curl			
Other_____			

Page 2

189

Cardio

Cardiovascular Exercise
Do your cardio three to five times a week.
(Choose one)
Bike; Bleachers; Elliptical; Sprints; Track; Treadmill; Other
Time / Duration:
MPH (speed):
Level:
Target Heart Rate:
 # Of Bleachers / Sprints:

Cardiovascular Exercise
Do your cardio three to five times a week.
(Choose one)
Bike; Bleachers; Elliptical; Sprints; Track; Treadmill; Other
Time / Duration:
MPH (speed):
Level:
Target Heart Rate:
 # Of Bleachers / Sprints:

Cardiovascular Exercise
Do your cardio three to five times a week.
(Choose one)
Bike; Bleachers; Elliptical; Sprints; Track; Treadmill; Other
Time / Duration:
MPH (speed):
Level:
Target Heart Rate:
 # Of Bleachers / Sprints:

Cardio

Cardiovascular Exercise
Do your cardio three to five times a week.
(Choose one)
Bike; Bleachers; Elliptical; Sprints; Track; Treadmill; Other
Time / Duration:
MPH (speed):
Level:
Target Heart Rate:
 # Of Bleachers / Sprints:

Cardiovascular Exercise
Do your cardio three to five times a week.
(Choose one)
Bike; Bleachers; Elliptical; Sprints; Track; Treadmill; Other
Time / Duration:
MPH (speed):
Level:
Target Heart Rate:
 # Of Bleachers / Sprints:

Chapter Nine

The Truth

...When he lies, he speaks his native language, for he is a liar and the father of lies

John 8:44

In the 1997 blockbuster hit *Liar Liar* Jim Carry plays a sycophantic, smooth-talking divorce attorney who has a propensity for propitious "prevarication" which makes him a success with all of his juries. Simply put, the guy's a great liar. However his five-year-old son Max can see through his lies (Matthew 11:25) and wants to see an end to them. So when his dad blows off his birthday bash with yet another weak excuse, Max wishes his dad could spend a whole day without lying. As his wish magically comes true the movie plays out with amusingly disastrous results in the courtroom. In true Hollywood fashion it easily makes light of something so serious.

But maybe we shouldn't take it so lightly. After all, deception is the root of all our problems.

Now there are different types of lies. There are subtle "white" lies, blatantly malicious lies, and even lies that appear harmless, or are in our minds even "justifiable" for the purpose of "protecting" someone else's feelings. But I'm not talking about any of these kinds of lies. The types I want to focus on are the not so obvious lies because they are the unspoken lies. I want to address the lies we repeatedly hear inside of our heads day in and day out.

Dictionary.com defines lying as something meant to deceive or give a wrong impression. I think many of us have the wrong impression of ourselves. We need to remember the truth which is....*So God created man in his own image, in the image of God he created him; male and female he created them.* (Genesis 1:27) Selah!

The truth is we were created wonderfully and beautifully, to be artistic, intelligent, strong, and healthy and to live life vivaciously. We were created in the image and likeness of God to rule and lead, to work and play. So if that is all true then why do so many of us feel ugly, fat, stupid, weak, and oppressed all the time?

It is because we hear lies and we believe them. It is because we don't give any attention whatsoever to the source of our "self talk". We hear thoughts in our head and we take ownership of them as if they are all really 100% true. And then, over a period of time, we ultimately live those thoughts (attitudes) out. We manifest those thoughts into reality. Everybody knows what I am talking about. Let me give you a personal example.

My alarm goes off every week day morning between 4:45 and 5 am (depending on how many times I hit snooze) and boom! As soon as I open my eyes I get engaged in an unwanted conversation. With me it goes something like this "man, I am so tired...I don't want to get out of bed and I definitely don't want to go to work this morning". But then I realize that is not the voice of God speaking through me. I realize that is a selfish lying spirit trying to oppress me *before my day even starts!* I realize that I am thankful for my warm bed my good night sleep, the job that I love and the job that provides for me and my family. So what do I do? I take captive that thought, realize it's not mine and then I consciously re-engage in the conversation which goes something like this... "God, thank you that I just had a pretty good night's sleep in a warm bed and that this morning I have a job to go to where people need me to be there for them to support them."

My response above is the correct biblical response too as we can see in 2 Corinthians 10:5. *We demolish arguments and every pretension that sets itself up against the knowledge of God, and <u>we take captive every thought</u> to make it obedient to Christ.*

We have to take capture of every thought that we have and ask ourselves what is the source of this? At first it may be kind of hard because there is a lot of chatter going on between our ears but over time it will get easier. Let me give you some basic guidelines and strategies for doing this, for discerning the truth that is. If you find yourself upset, annoyed, angry or experiencing any emotion other than peace, joy or love, then chances are you are believing the liar, who by the way is satan. Remember ...When *he (satan) lies, he speaks his native language, for he is a liar and the father of lies.*

In these following scenarios you should identify the lie but don't just stop there. Remember, you were created in the image of God so you should always <u>speak</u> like God would. You need to fight back by speaking the truth. That is why the word of God, *the Truth*, is referred to as "the s**word**", because it is actually a weapon against all deceit, lies, and falsehood.

Here are some very common and specific examples.

The lie you hear or say...I just can't quit smoking, the temptation is too strong!

The truth...1 Corinthians 10:13 *No temptation has seized you except what is common to man. And God is faithful; he will not let you be tempted beyond what you can bear. But when you are tempted, he will also provide a way out so that you can stand up under it.*

The lie you hear or say...I am fat and I will never lose this weight because I don't have any self control when it comes to eating!

The truth...2 Timothy 1:7 *For God did not give us a spirit of timidity, but a spirit of power, of love and of self-discipline.*

The lie you hear or say...I'll never be able to get rid of all my debt!

The truth...Philippians 4:19 *And my God will meet all your needs according to his glorious riches in Christ Jesus.*

The lie you hear or say...God will never forgive me for _____.

The truth...**Psalm 103:12-13** *as far as the east is from the west, so far has he removed our transgressions from us. As a father has compassion on his children, so the Lord has compassion on those who fear him;*

When I further think about the concept of hearing the voice of God and discerning the truth I am reminded of the 1971 Memorex campaign that launched Recordable Audio Cassettes. It was one of the most memorable campaigns in television history. The image of Ella Fitzgerald's recorded voice shattering a wine glass was seen and remembered by millions and the accompanying theme line, "Is it live or is it Memorex?," was quickly adopted by mainstream America. 32 years later, the phrase is useful to us on a spiritual level. We need to ask ourselves the same question, *"Is it live, or is it Memorex?"*

Let me give you some more examples. You may also hear things like,

1. "your boss is a jerk."
2. "your spouse doesn't love you anymore because they haven't been doing those nice things they used to do."
3. "your child is intentionally doing that just to make you angry and defy your authority."

Well I can tell you by the negative content of each of those statements that they are some cheap recorded voice that you have probably heard playing between your ears more than once. If it was live...the living voice of God, then those comments would have sounded something more like this...

1. "your boss treated you like that because he doesn't know how to effectively communicate the stress that he is under and He needs your *support* right now while he gets through whatever issues he is facing...you should talk to him about it."

2. "your significant other stopped doing the things they used to do because they are sending a subconscious signal that they are unhappy about something in the relationship...you should talk to them about it."

3. "your child is behaving that way because something is wrong and they are trying to get your attention...you should talk to them about it."

The major difference between those two sets of voices is that one is coming from of place of selfishness and anger while the other is coming from a place of selflessness and love.

We need to understand that not every voice we hear is a good one to listen to. The reality of it is, unless it is God's voice in between your ears you should probably ignore it. I know what my own voice sounds like and I usually end up getting myself into trouble if I listen to it. Instead I listen for the voice of God.

If what is being said is loving, then I know it is Him, I know it is the *Truth*!

Some of you maybe thinking I have never heard the voice of God, I don't know what it sounds like. You maybe asking is it an audible voice? I know that before I learned to distinguish the voice of God I used to ask my Christian mentors the same question. What does His voice sound like? Is it audible? Is it thunderous? I don't want to put limitations on God but He usually speaks to me quietly and inside of me to where no one else can hear what He is saying, which brings me to another point.

If you want to hear the live voice of God sometimes you have to be in a quiet place. If you never have down time in a secret quiet place where you go to pray that could be an obstacle in your ability to hear His voice.

Another example that I could give you is when you get a phone call from a stranger and you don't recognize the voice. If it was a family member or friend calling, you would recognize it because you are used to hearing their voice. It's the same with God...if He is familiar to you...then you will recognize Him when He speaks.

Another way to know the voice (truth) of God is to know the word of God. I have found that as I have read the bible more I have actually begun remembering the scriptures. Now I am not talking about verbatim with exact chapters and verses but I am talking about the general content. Often times I will be talking to myself or asking myself a question and the answer will come in the form of a scripture that I hear in my head. That too is God speaking His word into my specific situation. He is telling me the truth.

Also, an extremely important part of hearing God's voice and learning the truth is doing what it says. What good is being able to hear His voice if you don't act on what He is saying? This point is made very clearly when Jesus said, *My sheep listen to my voice; I know them, and they follow me.* (John 10:27)

You see, he didn't just say that they listen, but that they follow! I think a lot of casual Christians deceive themselves and are going to be surprised when it is all over and done with. They will be in line waiting to get into heaven and when Jesus walks by they are going to throw their hand up to give Him a high five only to receive a bewildered look from Him in return. With a confused look on His face He will say *"...I never knew you. Away from me, you evildoers!"* (Matthew 7:23)

We know that we have come to know him if we obey his commands. *The man who says, "I know him," but does not do what he commands is a liar, and the truth is not in him.* (1 John 2:3-4) Claiming belief in God and Jesus is easy and many will be saved...but obedience to and living the truth are completely different and much harder.

Hollywood movies are great for lessons on the truth because all of us like to be entertained more than we like to learn. In another blockbuster hit, and a personal favorite of mine, we hear Jack Nicholson say *"You can't handle the Truth!"* during a heated courtroom cross examination. While I don't necessarily agree with Jack Nicholson's idea of what the truth is in the movie "A Few Good Men", I do agree with his statement. Most people can't handle the truth because the truth often hurts (suffering).

I remember very clearly the night the truth was revealed to me. I could not eat or sleep for weeks, in fact, I would just as soon not have been apart of this world. Since that time, my reality has guided me to the understanding that the discovery of Truth, about who we are and why we are here, leads us to a certain but exact death; only to be followed by a whole new life, in which we are called to the infantile task of learning how to live again, but in a paradoxes paradigm that not everyone else is privy to. I know that was a mouthful so here it is again...

...the discovery of Truth, about who we are and why we are here, leads us to a certain and exact death; only to be followed by a whole new life, in which we are called to the infantile task of learning how to live again, but in a paradoxes paradigm that not everyone else is privy to.

Let me elaborate. One of the first manifestations of Truth is a state of brokenness. We feel broken the minute we realize we have been living in a state of self deception. Examples could include the discovery that we have been neglecting our body for years, even decades, to the point of debilitated health and diminished self esteem. Or what about the discovery that we have been neglecting our marriages or worse yet violating the covenants we made to our spouse because we falsely believed we were entitled to something better. Or what about the discovery that the false security we put into our stock portfolio is gone with the blink of an eye because evil inevitably flourished in some dark corporate office in a city far from the safety of the well lit and private community that we live in. The bible gives us perspective on this brokenness and exposure in a sense of our lives coming forth into the light.

Everyone who does evil hates the light, and will not come into the light for fear that his deeds will be exposed. But whoever lives by the **truth** *comes into the light, so that it may be seen plainly that what he has done has been done through God.*(John 3:20-21)

Many people are afraid to come into the light because they fear their brokenness will be exposed (no courage). They also do not want to be changed because of the pain that inexorably accompanies it (suffering). If you yourself are blessed with the experience of coming to the light, i.e. a revelation of the Truth, do not be at all surprised if you receive *resistance* or rejection from those around you, even from your closest family members. Often time's people resent your acknowledgment of the truth because they fear it will expose some of the darkness in their lives.

As terrible as the truth may be sounding right now, it is not! The truth is not only a gift from God, but also a tool for us. Thus we should receive it as such, for it is written in…*And I will ask the Father, and he will give you another Counselor to be with you forever—the Spirit of* **truth**. *The world cannot accept him, because it neither sees him nor knows him. But you know him, for he lives with you and will be in you.* (John 14:16-17)

Our secular world would have us believe that we all have a conscious that helps us discern between what is right and what is wrong. The medical or scientific term, "conscious", in my opinion is a clever undermining of not only the evidence that the Holy Spirit of Christ lives and dwells in us but also of the infinite wisdom and discerning power that we bear from His spirit of Truth.

Once we have acknowledged our brokenness, and the world's for that matter, it is only then that we can begin the process of healing. We begin by examining our past behaviors and the emotions and *the lies* that caused those behaviors. We frantically search with Hope and Faith for the only alternative to the previous deception that once clouded our vision of what was best for our lives. That may mean forgiving others, forgiving ourselves, changing habits, changing environments, and often times even the people that we spend our time with.

Healing and constantly living in the truth takes a deep commitment. It is not a quick process and there is no exact formula. The healing process is also a lonely time. As your desire for the truth grows, God takes you to a place, often times to a desert place which will discuss in chapter 11, where money, other people, jobs, or relationships cannot distract you from what it is He wants you to learn. It is in that desert place that God teaches you who He is and how much He loves you as He sets you free. *To the Jews who had believed him (disciples), Jesus said, "If you hold to my teaching (discipline), you are really my disciples. Then you will know the truth, and the truth will set you free."* (John 8:31-32)

Thus we arrive at the pinnacle of the revelation of truth, its purification in your life, and the pursuing walk in it, which is freedom. You receive the freedom to live like you never have before, a freedom to live without fear, pride, guilt, anger, jealousy, and hate; a freedom to live in new grace, a constant state of not only receiving but also giving forgiveness. Most importantly you receive the freedom to live in a state of love...agape love. We are told in 1 Peter 1:22 *Now that you have purified yourselves by obeying the truth so that you have sincere love for your brothers, love one another deeply, from the heart.*

Think about the people in your life; the past and the present. What were they like? What are they like now? Was there someone in your life who was previously physically or verbally abusive toward you but now they treat you with love, peace and respect? Is there a friend of yours who used to smoke, get intoxicated habitually, or use drugs who no longer does those things? Is there someone in your life who used to be grossly overweight who has since lost that weight and became healthy again? Of course there are people like this all around us. I am one of those people!

We have been restored! We have found and been set free by the truth! We are more like Jesus today than we were yesterday. We are more like the Son of God this year than we were last year. By faith we had a revelation of who we were. By faith we accepted the unmerited favor and grace of God as we pursued Him and the things of Him and what was written about Him in the Hebrew Scriptures and the New Testament. We took hold of the truth, we ate it...

See how this all works together? The truth is, you are going to be lied to every day for the rest of your life and most of us are even lying to ourselves. You can believe what you want and go through life oppressed and in the role of a victim or you can learn the truth, which is the word of God, and use it like a warrior to navigate you to your destiny, the desire of your heart according to God's will for your life. Finding the truth, and walking in the truth are essential in achieving great spiritual and physical health.

Chapter/Week Nine
Spiritual Workout

1. When you think of yourself or talk to yourself are you mostly positive or negative? What negative thing do you most often say or think about yourself?

_____

_____

_____

_____

_____

_____

_____

_____

2. What is the statement and scripture that counters your negative thoughts or speech and reminds you of the truth?

_____

_____

_____

_____

_____

_____

_____

_____

_____

3. Why do people avoid the truth and are you avoiding any areas of truth in your life?

_____

_____

_____

_____

_____

_____

_____

_____

_____

_____

4. What does John 8:32 say about the truth and what area of your life can you apply that to?

_____

_____

_____

_____

_____

_____

_____

_____

5. What does Jesus say about those who know the truth but do not live it?

_____

_____

_____

_____

_____

_____

_____

_____

Workout 1

Always: Warm-up with an eight- ten minute light cardiovascular exercise of choice, then start with a warm-up set using fifty percent of what you will be lifting on your first set and also stretch between sets. Fill in the chart below by selecting an exercise from each muscle group and filling in the pounds you lifted for each repetition.

(Choose one)

Exercises	Reps	Lbs.	Rest (Min.)
THIGHS (P)			
Leg Press	Set 1: 13-15	_____	1
Squats	Set 2: 10-12	_____	1
Leg Extensions	Set 3: 8-10	_____	1
Stationary Lunge	Set 4: 6-8	_____	1
Step Ups	Set 5: 20	_____	0
Ball Squat			
Other_____			
CORE ABS			
Flat Crunch	_____		0.5
Twist Floor Crunch			
Incline Crunch			
Leg Raise			
Twisting Ball Crunch			
Ball Rollouts			
Other_____			
CHEST (P)			
Flat Bench Press	Set 1: 13-15	_____	1
Incline Bench Press	Set 2: 10-12	_____	1
Machine Press	Set 3: 8-10	_____	1
Dumbbell Fly	Set 4: 6-8	_____	1
Push Ups	Set 5: 20	_____	0
Dumbbell/Ball Press			
Dumbbell/Ball Fly			
Other_____			

Page 1

206

Workout 1

(Choose one)

Exercises	Reps	Lbs.	Rest (Min.)
CORE ABS			
Flat Crunch	_____		0.5
Twist Floor Crunch			
Incline Crunch			
Leg Raise			
Twisting Ball Crunch			
Ball Rollouts			
Other _____			
SHOULDERS (S)			
Dumbbell Press	Set 1: 13-15	_____	1
Machine Press	Set 2: 10-12	_____	1
Dumbbell Side Raise	Set 3: 8-10	_____	1
Dumbbell Rear Squeeze	Set 4: 6-8	_____	1
Dumbbell/Ball Press	Set 5: 20	_____	0
Band Side Raise			
Other _____			
CORE ABS			
Flat Crunch	_____		0.5
Twist Floor Crunch			
Incline Crunch			
Leg Raise			
Twisting Ball Crunch			
Ball Rollouts			
Other _____			
TRICEPS- ARMS (S)			
Tricep Pushdown	Set 1: 13-15	_____	1
French Curls	Set 2: 10-12	_____	1
Rope Pushdowns	Set 3: 8-10	_____	1
One Arm Pushdowns	Set 4: 6-8	_____	1
Chair Dips	Set 5: 20	_____	0
Dumbbell/Ball Kickbacks			
Other _____			

Page 2

207

Workout 2

Always: Warm-up with an eight- ten minute light cardiovascular exercise of choice, then start with a warm-up set using fifty percent of what you will be lifting on your first set and also stretch between sets. Fill in the chart below by selecting an exercise from each muscle group and filling in the pounds you lifted for each repetition.

(Choose one)

Exercises	Reps	Lbs.	Rest (Min.)
BACK OF THIGH (P)			
Laying Leg Curls	Set 1: 13-15	_____	1
Dumbbell Dead Lifts	Set 2: 10-12	_____	1
Reverse Lunge	Set 3: 8-10	_____	1
Stationary Lunge	Set 4: 6-8	_____	1
Ball Curls	Set 5: 20	_____	0
Dumbbell Leg Curls			
Other_____			
CORE ABS			
Flat Crunch	_____		0.5
Twist Floor Crunch			
Incline Crunch			
Leg Raise			
Twisting Ball Crunch			
Ball Rollouts			
Other_____			
CALVES (P)			
Standing Raise	Set 1: 13-15	_____	1
Seated Raise	Set 2: 10-12	_____	1
Leg Press	Set 3: 8-10	_____	1
One Leg Raise	Set 4: 6-8	_____	1
Two Leg Dumbbell Raise	Set 5: 20	_____	0
Other_____			

Page 1

208

Workout 2

(Choose one)

Exercises	Reps	Lbs.	Rest (Min.)
CORE ABS			
Flat Crunch	——		0.5
Twist Floor Crunch			
Incline Crunch			
Leg Raise			
Twisting Ball Crunch			
Ball Rollouts			
Other_____			

Exercises	Reps	Lbs.	Rest (Min.)
BACK (P)			
Straight Bar Pull Down	Set 1: 13-15	____	1
Close Grip Pull	Set 2: 10-12	____	1
Seated Row	Set 3: 8-10	____	1
Reverse Grip Pull Down	Set 4: 6-8	____	1
Dumbbell Row	Set 5: 20	____	0
Band/Desk Row			
Two Arm Dumbbell Row			
Other_____			

Exercises	Reps	Lbs.	Rest (Min.)
CORE ABS			
Flat Crunch	——		0.5
Twist Floor Crunch			
Incline Crunch			
Leg Raise			
Twisting Ball Crunch			
Ball Rollouts			
Other_____			

Exercises	Reps	Lbs.	Rest (Min.)
BICEPS- ARMS (S)			
Dumbbell Curl	Set 1: 13-15	____	1
Barbell Curls	Set 2: 10-12	____	1
Barbell Preacher Curls	Set 3: 8-10	____	1
Dumbbell Hammer Curl	Set 4: 6-8	____	1
Dumbbell/Ball Seated Curl	Set 5: 20	____	0
Dumbbell/Ball Preacher Curl			
Other_____			

Page 2

209

Workout 1

Always: Warm-up with an eight- ten minute light cardiovascular exercise of choice, then start with a warm-up set using fifty percent of what you will be lifting on your first set and also stretch between sets. Fill in the chart below by selecting an exercise from each muscle group and filling in the pounds you lifted for each repetition.

(Choose one)

Exercises	Reps	Lbs.	Rest (Min.)
THIGHS (P)			
Leg Press	Set 1: 13-15	_____	1
Squats	Set 2: 10-12	_____	1
Leg Extensions	Set 3: 8-10	_____	1
Stationary Lunge	Set 4: 6-8	_____	1
Step Ups	Set 5: 20	_____	0
Ball Squat			
Other_____			
CORE ABS			
Flat Crunch	_____		0.5
Twist Floor Crunch			
Incline Crunch			
Leg Raise			
Twisting Ball Crunch			
Ball Rollouts			
Other_____			
CHEST (P)			
Flat Bench Press	Set 1: 13-15	_____	1
Incline Bench Press	Set 2: 10-12	_____	1
Machine Press	Set 3: 8-10	_____	1
Dumbbell Fly	Set 4: 6-8	_____	1
Push Ups	Set 5: 20	_____	0
Dumbbell/Ball Press			
Dumbbell/Ball Fly			
Other_____			

Page 1

Workout 1

(Choose one)

Exercises	Reps	Lbs.	Rest (Min.)
CORE ABS			
Flat Crunch	_____		0.5
Twist Floor Crunch			
Incline Crunch			
Leg Raise			
Twisting Ball Crunch			
Ball Rollouts			
Other_____			
SHOULDERS (S)			
Dumbbell Press	Set 1: 13-15	_____	1
Machine Press	Set 2: 10-12	_____	1
Dumbbell Side Raise	Set 3: 8-10	_____	1
Dumbbell Rear Squeeze	Set 4: 6-8	_____	1
Dumbbell/Ball Press	Set 5: 20	_____	0
Band Side Raise			
Other_____			
CORE ABS			
Flat Crunch	_____		0.5
Twist Floor Crunch			
Incline Crunch			
Leg Raise			
Twisting Ball Crunch			
Ball Rollouts			
Other_____			
TRICEPS- ARMS (S)			
Tricep Pushdown	Set 1: 13-15	_____	1
French Curls	Set 2: 10-12	_____	1
Rope Pushdowns	Set 3: 8-10	_____	1
One Arm Pushdowns	Set 4: 6-8	_____	1
Chair Dips	Set 5: 20	_____	0
Dumbbell/Ball Kickbacks			
Other_____			

Page 2

211

Cardio

Cardiovascular Exercise
Do your cardio three to five times a week.
(Choose one)
Bike; Bleachers; Elliptical; Sprints; Track; Treadmill; Other
Time / Duration:
MPH (speed):
Level:
Target Heart Rate:
 # Of Bleachers / Sprints:

Cardiovascular Exercise
Do your cardio three to five times a week.
(Choose one)
Bike; Bleachers; Elliptical; Sprints; Track; Treadmill; Other
Time / Duration:
MPH (speed):
Level:
Target Heart Rate:
 # Of Bleachers / Sprints:

Cardiovascular Exercise
Do your cardio three to five times a week.
(Choose one)
Bike; Bleachers; Elliptical; Sprints; Track; Treadmill; Other
Time / Duration:
MPH (speed):
Level:
Target Heart Rate:
 # Of Bleachers / Sprints:

Page 1

Cardio

Cardiovascular Exercise
Do your cardio three to five times a week.
(Choose one)
Bike; Bleachers; Elliptical; Sprints; Track; Treadmill; Other
Time / Duration:
MPH (speed):
Level:
Target Heart Rate:
 # Of Bleachers / Sprints:

Cardiovascular Exercise
Do your cardio three to five times a week.
(Choose one)
Bike; Bleachers; Elliptical; Sprints; Track; Treadmill; Other
Time / Duration:
MPH (speed):
Level:
Target Heart Rate:
 # Of Bleachers / Sprints:

Chapter Ten

Self-Image

The past is not simply the past, but a prism through which the subject filters his own changing self-image.

Doris Kearns Goodwin

Although I am not a gambling man, I would be willing to bet that when most of us think about our past we tend to gravitate towards the things we would have liked to have done differently...things that we regret. Even worse, some of us probably experience shameful feelings of guilt and un-forgiveness that stem from our past. This is important to recognize because a person's positive self image is hindered primarily by those two things; guilt and un-forgiveness.

With that revelation it is no wonder it seems everywhere I go I see or hear the words..."Extreme Makeover". Everybody wants a new image. We've got the extreme makeover television show for people's bodies and self images. We've got the extreme makeover television show for people's homes. We had the extreme makeover theme going on in our Church for single moms on Mother's day. I even caught the tail end of a sermon series on the radio with an extreme makeover theme. It's just like our world and society to hop on a band wagon. As I observe all of this I wonder why would any of us even need an extreme makeover since we were all created in the healthiest image of God?

People so often think that if they can just lose weight, enlarge their breasts, enhance their muscles, fix their smiles and remove their physical faults that they will look more attractive to the world and then they will be happy because of the world's admiration of them. This idea may be true, but it is shallow and does not last. I have seen it over and over and over again. In fact I have experienced it myself. And what about the woman who is so beautiful that the world never sees anything else in or about her? The world is so busy admiring or lusting over her beauty that nothing else is ever expected from or appreciated about her. It didn't always used to be like this. Peter addresses beauty and tells us how it used to and should still be. *Instead, it should be that of your inner self, the unfading beauty of a gentle and quiet spirit, which is of great worth in God's sight. For this is the way the holy women of the past who put their hope in God used to make themselves beautiful.* (1 Peter 3:4-5)

It is a travesty, perhaps even a sin that we place so much emphasis on our physical nature when it is our spiritual nature that makes us who we are. If somebody really wants an extreme makeover they are not going to find it in a plastic surgeon's office, but they can find it in Christ...and it is free. *Therefore, if anyone is in Christ, he is a new creation; the old has gone, the new has come!* (2 Corinthians 5:17)

When a person accepts Jesus Christ as their personal savior, and believes that He was the Son of God who died for their sins, they under go a transformation that results in an entirely new being. Creation takes place again as the Holy Spirit inculcates their body with the eternal life of God. *But now he has reconciled you by Christ's physical body through death to present you holy in his sight, without blemish and free from accusation* (Colossians 1:22)

We have all been witnesses to extreme makeovers happening in the lives of those around us. There's the son who doesn't drink or do drugs anymore. There's the daughter or brother who quit smoking. There's the husband who became gentle and the wife who transformed her health. We see these types of extreme makeovers all the time and then we get to hear about them too. *"Oh, Jesus delivered me from this...Jesus delivered me from that."* I'll bet some of my non-believing clients are sick of hearing about this Jesus guy that gave me my extreme makeover. But it can't be helped. You see the second part of the earlier passage goes like this...*All this (the extreme makeover and new life) is from God, who reconciled us to himself through Christ and gave us the ministry of reconciliation:* (2 Corinthians 5:18)

You see, these extreme makeovers do not come alone but with a responsibility and a desire. Anyone who receives a life transformation is "reconciled" with God and with that comes the desire to share what they now know and share what they now have. Everyone deserves to be free from their addictions, forgiven for their embarrassing and shameful pasts, and free to follow the dreams and desires of their hearts.

To those outside the church and to those who don't have a relationship with Christ this is non-sense so I will once again show you the reflection of a spiritual principle with a description of a physical one to explain how and why this new creation takes place. In ancient times goatskins were used to hold wine. As the fresh grape juice fermented, the wine would expand, and the new wineskin would stretch. But a used skin, already stretched, would break. When you enter into a relationship with Jesus, it's the same. He brings a newness that cannot be confined within the old forms. You cannot put the

Holy Spirit in an unholy body or it will burst. The body has to be cleansed, sanctified. Jesus explained this when He said, *"Neither do men pour new wine into old wineskins. If they do, the skins will burst, the wine will run out and the wineskins will be ruined. No, they pour new wine into new wineskins, and both are preserved."* (Matthew 9:17)

So for once the media is right on about something...we all need extreme makeovers...the spiritual kind that comes from entering into a relationship with Jesus Christ. But as I mentioned earlier, one of the things that keeps us from having a positive self-image and allowing God to give us an extreme makeover are feelings of guilt and un-forgiveness.

"Guilty" was the word heard four times in a row as the verdict came back in the 2004 Martha Stewart trial. As the words rang through the air, undoubtedly following there would be consequences (accountability and discipline) for all who were involved with her, including the innocent investors in her company. But probably none would feel greater consequences than Martha, both inside her heart and soul. Sure, as a society we have a judicial system in place to govern us and it serves its purpose, fallibly. But individually, we've been given an un-arguable and un-deniable "system" to govern ourselves as well.

You see, guilt is a human emotion derived from a built in moral compass that helps govern our morality. From the very beginning of human existence we can see the characteristics of guilt. The first is that guilt never likes to be alone. The original example of this is seen when Eve felt the burden of her rebellion against God. She sought to involve Adam in the sharing of that burden. But who is to say Adam was not already experiencing his own guilt for not acting like a man and for not correcting, i.e. *telling the truth*, to both the serpent and Eve in their discussion of the fruit. After all, it was Adam's responsibility, he was the one put in charge. The second characteristic of guilt is the need to hide it. As the two of them experienced guilt, together, they attempted to hide from God.

It's kind of funny when you think about it. Here we are as an evolved society with all of our technological advances and all of our science but yet 6000 years later we are all still acting the same way emotionally. We do something wrong, we feel guilty, and then we attempt to cover it up. Some of us are good at covering it up so the rest of the world doesn't see. But God always sees, we cannot hide anything from Him and we know it...thus the feeling of guilt! But then there are those people who couldn't care less and make no effort to cover up their moral indiscretions. I should point out though, that the absence of guilt does not imply that you are necessarily doing something right. In other cases, many times people break God's moral laws out of ignorance because they only have the very basic religious "concepts" to go by and do not really know what the actual moral code is according to God and the bible. In addition, after we repeatedly commit the same sin over and over again that moral compass in our heart begins to harden and we get to a point of numbness where we can no longer even feel any guilt.

With all of that understood, we now need to ask ourselves this very important question. To what extent does guilt help or hurt us? Guilt can be a good thing. I once knew a woman who loved to say..."guilt is a gift you give yourself", meaning, each of us can decide what we are going to feel guilty about and what we will not. This woman wasn't much of a biblical scholar though and didn't know that guilt is actually derived from a gift given to us from God. You see, one of God's gifts to believers was the Holy Sprit. And we know that one of the functions of the Holy Spirit was to convict the world of guilt...*When he (the Holy Spirit) comes, he will convict the world of guilt in regard to sin and righteousness and judgment:* (John 16:8)

So, I say guilt is a good thing to the extent that it makes me desire to live Godly, according to the standards of the Holy Spirit living inside of me. I say it is also a good thing because it puts all of us in the same boat. Am I any better than Charlie Manson or Adolph Hitler? By the world's judicial system, yeah,

I am like Mother Teresa compared to those two guys. But I can't be led by the world's judicial system. I have to remember that I am just as guilty as those guys and I am reminded of that when I read, *...for all have sinned and fall short of the glory of God, and are justified freely by his grace through the redemption that came by Christ Jesus* (Romans 3:23-24)

The same grace and forgiveness that is available to me is or was available to them. I know, I don't exactly understand it either but it is what it is whether we understand it or not.

Now, at the same time, a normal and healthy emotion like guilt, which was intended to guide us, can also be grossly perverted so that it encumbers us. So get this next point because this is the crux of this entire message; when our sins are forgiven...SO SHOULD OUR FEELINGS OF GUILT. If you have asked God for forgiveness for a sin that you have truly repented of it, meaning you have stopped committing it, then you should also be relieved of the feelings of guilt that were associated with it. If you are still feeling guilt, then you are being oppressed; you are being lied to with thoughts that are telling you you're not really forgiven. We know that guilt is forgiven with sins because we read it in Psalm 32:5...*Then I acknowledged my sin to you and did not cover up (hide) my iniquity. I said, "I will confess my transgressions to the Lord"-- and you forgave the guilt of my sin.*

David clearly acknowledges that because he did not *hide*, God also forgave the guilt of his sin. Both the *sin* and the *guilt of the sin* are distinguishably separable. Further more, in the next verse, John addresses the fact that we are sometimes particularly and unnecessarily hard on ourselves having the tendency to feel condemned and un-forgiven in our hearts. But we can put our hearts at rest because God is greater than our hearts and because He can judge us more accurately than we can judge ourselves. *This then is how we know that we belong to the truth, and how we set our hearts at rest in his presence whenever our hearts condemn us.*

For God is greater than our hearts, and he knows everything. (1 John 3:19-21)

Trust me when I tell you, nothing you can do, and nothing you are feeling guilty about is worse than what Paul did. He was a **murderer** and God forgave him *of his guilt* so much that he was able to write many of the books in the New Testament. So maybe you committed adultery in your youth, maybe you got divorced, maybe you did drugs, maybe you stole something, lied to somebody, maybe you have neglected your health or your family, only you know why you carry the burden of guilt. But chances are you have already been punished or punished yourself enough for your mistakes...*so the guilt is no longer necessary.* Only you can believe what the bible says about your past and your future. And this is what the bible says; *Therefore, there is now no condemnation for those who are in Christ Jesus, because through Christ Jesus the law of the Spirit of life set me free from the law of sin and death.* (Romans 8:1)

Believing you are forgiven and believing what God says about you, as opposed to what other people say about you and as opposed to what you say or think about yourself, is the only thing that matters. This understanding is fundamental in developing a healthy self image and greater physical and spiritual health.

Now let's look at the other side of the coin. People can also have *too much* pride and self image. Here we are getting into vanity and arrogance. This is just as harmful to your spiritual health as guilt. This is what God does to the arrogant...*Your heart became proud on account of your beauty, and you corrupted your wisdom because of your splendor. So I threw you to the earth; I made a spectacle of you before kings. By your many sins and dishonest trade you have desecrated your sanctuaries. So I made a fire come out from you, and it consumed you, and I reduced you to ashes on the ground in the sight of all who were watching.* (Ezekiel 28:17-18)

When I think of vanity, pride and arrogance I remember the line, *"Help me! Help you!"* from the movie Jerry Maguire. With great frustration, those were the words of Tom Cruise to Cuba Gooding Jr.

In this movie Tom Cruise played a self-absorbed, *arrogant* sports agent who lost his job after having had a moral epiphany. His only remaining client was Cuba Gooding Jr. who also played an *arrogant*, obnoxious and self-absorbed NFL wide receiver who was intensely concerned with getting his multi-million dollar contract along with all the fame that comes from being a professional athlete; so much that he was a maverick and did not understand the concept of a "team" (support).

Both of these men were at points in their lives where they wanted change. They wanted something better for themselves but they could not attain want they wanted without help. Their lofty self-image was hindering their spiritual, physical, and even financial growth. Their selfishness, pride, vanity and arrogant egos were preventing them from receiving the blessings of love, peace, and greater prosperity. How many of us act the same way as these two men?

Often times I have felt like Jerry Maguire when helping my clients try to claim their blessings for better health. Frustration has occasionally set in when clients have expressed intense desires to lose weight or inches and reshape their bodies but yet they still eat exactly the opposite of the way that they should and they consciously decide not to exercise their biblical responsibility to perform cardiovascular exercise. It is flat out arrogant rebellion to all the things that God stands for and all the things they know they should be doing.

However, when this frustration does set in, it never lasts because I always remind myself that I am dealing with human beings like myself who are also prone to denial, justification, and self-destructive behavior. I also remind myself that I am not their ultimate source and that they must choose to rely on God for the changes they are seeking. I so often in my own life have to rely on the words of David as he reminds us, *"Our* help *is in the name of the Lord, the Maker of heaven and earth.* (Psalm 124:8)

I have found that some people are eager to rely on God as they pursue better health while others are not. I can only imagine that God himself at times would also like to scream out to the entire planet "Help me! Help you!" But He does not. In reality God can do what ever he wants without any help at all as we see from this passage in Isaiah. *I looked, but there was no one to* help, *I was appalled that no one gave* **support***; so my own arm worked salvation for me, and my own wrath sustained me.* (Isaiah 63:5)

You have probably heard the saying that God only helps those who help themselves. This is not exactly true because everyone on the entire planet, whether a believer or not, is living under the grace of God for the time being. However, to a degree the statement is true. I believe that God's greatest blessings do go to those who help themselves. How does God want us to help ourselves and Him? Here are six ways we can help God help us. By simply believing in Him; by being *humble* and admitting our need for Him. By diligently seeking the answers to our prayers from the bible. By patiently being willing to wait for Him to change us on the inside instead of just our circumstances on the outside. By tithing consistently every week no matter what challenges we are faced with financially. And lastly by praising Him and not complaining, regardless of our circumstances.

Continuing on, along the same lines of vanity, not too many years ago I decided I needed to lose some weight myself. Now anyone who knows me personally is probably thinking that is my dry sense of humor because I am 5'10" and only 200 pounds, but I assure you it is not humor, I am serious. My arrogance and vanity was causing me undue burdens that I had to carry around like a bunch of unwanted body fat. My higher than required self-image was a strain on my business relationships as well as all of my personal relationships. Sin in general will cause undue burden whether it is vanity, lack of discipline, sexual impurity or anything else you can think of. Think I am crazy? Then the author of Hebrews must have been crazy too when he wrote, *Therefore we also, since we are surrounded by so great a cloud of witnesses, let us lay aside every weight, and the sin which so easily ensnares us, and let us run with endurance the race that is set before us.*(Hebrews 12:1)

The type of weight we're talking about is the heaviness that comes from inside of us when we know our lifestyles are not consistent with what we inherently know is best for us. We all have that small nagging voice, that nagging feeling, that nagging *something* that we can't always put a finger on but we know it is weighing us down. It is keeping us from a healthy self-image.

It is absolutely fundamental for all us to understand that not only our obedience but also our sins are each determined by what we believe and what we feel inside of our hearts. *For it is with your heart that you believe and are justified...* (Romans 10:10) Over the years, through my own personal experiences, through observing my clients, and through divine revelation I have come to understand that when a person wants to lose physical body weight they first have to lose the weight internally. They have to lose the sin and guilt. Sin and guilt adversely affect our self image and the only way to lose sin and guilt is to *humble* ourselves before God. There is no room in the Kingdom for arrogance or vanity.

To summarize this chapter, we have to know who we are, and what we are, which is no more and no less than what God says about us. As the quote says in the beginning of this chapter, we can all use the past as a prism to see our changing self-image. However, we don't need to look to our own past, but to the past of Jesus Christ because i*t is through His past that we can all acquire a healthy image of God!*

For another great program entirely on self worth I highly recommend reading "The Search for Significance"

Chapter/Week Ten
Spiritual Workout

1. What are the two primary things that keep people from having a healthy self-image?

   _____

   _____

   _____

   _____

   _____

   _____

   _____

2. For what do you feel guilty and why? Have you repented (stopped) the thing you feel guilty of? Ask God to forgive you and then believe it is done.

   _____

   _____

   _____

   _____

   _____

   _____

   _____

   _____

3. Do you need to forgive anyone in your life? Write it down and if appropriate, tell the person that you forgive them. Why is it important to forgive others?

   _____

   _____

   _____

_____

_____

_____

_____

_____

_____

4. How do you feel about the way your body looks? If it is not a healthy feeling then what are you doing to both spiritually and physically change this?

_____

_____

_____

_____

_____

_____

_____

_____

5. How does God view you and how are you supposed to view yourself?

_____

_____

_____

_____

_____

_____

_____

_____

Workout 2

Always: Warm-up with an eight- ten minute light cardiovascular exercise of choice, then start with a warm-up set using fifty percent of what you will be lifting on your first set and also stretch between sets. Fill in the chart below by selecting an exercise from each muscle group and filling in the pounds you lifted for each repetition.

(Choose one)

Exercises	Reps	Lbs.	Rest (Min.)
BACK OF THIGH (P)			
Laying Leg Curls	Set 1: 13-15	_____	1
Dumbbell Dead Lifts	Set 2: 10-12	_____	1
Reverse Lunge	Set 3: 8-10	_____	1
Stationary Lunge	Set 4: 6-8	_____	1
Ball Curls	Set 5: 20	_____	0
Dumbbell Leg Curls			
Other_____			
CORE ABS			
Flat Crunch	_____		0.5
Twist Floor Crunch			
Incline Crunch			
Leg Raise			
Twisting Ball Crunch			
Ball Rollouts			
Other_____			
CALVES (P)			
Standing Raise	Set 1: 13-15	_____	1
Seated Raise	Set 2: 10-12	_____	1
Leg Press	Set 3: 8-10	_____	1
One Leg Raise	Set 4: 6-8	_____	1
Two Leg Dumbbell Raise	Set 5: 20	_____	0
Other_____			

Page 1

228

Workout 2

(Choose one)

Exercises	Reps	Lbs.	Rest (Min.)
CORE ABS			
Flat Crunch	_____		0.5
Twist Floor Crunch			
Incline Crunch			
Leg Raise			
Twisting Ball Crunch			
Ball Rollouts			
Other_____			

BACK (P)			
Straight Bar Pull Down	Set 1: 13-15	_____	1
Close Grip Pull	Set 2: 10-12	_____	1
Seated Row	Set 3: 8-10	_____	1
Reverse Grip Pull Down	Set 4: 6-8	_____	1
Dumbbell Row	Set 5: 20	_____	0
Band/Desk Row			
Two Arm Dumbbell Row			
Other_____			

CORE ABS			
Flat Crunch	_____		0.5
Twist Floor Crunch			
Incline Crunch			
Leg Raise			
Twisting Ball Crunch			
Ball Rollouts			
Other_____			

BICEPS- ARMS (S)			
Dumbbell Curl	Set 1: 13-15	_____	1
Barbell Curls	Set 2: 10-12	_____	1
Barbell Preacher Curls	Set 3: 8-10	_____	1
Dumbbell Hammer Curl	Set 4: 6-8	_____	1
Dumbbell/Ball Seated Curl	Set 5: 20	_____	0
Dumbbell/Ball Preacher Curl			
Other_____			

Page 2

229

Workout 1

Always: Warm-up with an eight- ten minute light cardiovascular exercise of choice, then start with a warm-up set using fifty percent of what you will be lifting on your first set and also stretch between sets. Fill in the chart below by selecting an exercise from each muscle group and filling in the pounds you lifted for each repetition.

(Choose one)

Exercises	Reps	Lbs.	Rest (Min.)
THIGHS (P)			
Leg Press	Set 1: 13-15	_____	1
Squats	Set 2: 10-12	_____	1
Leg Extensions	Set 3: 8-10	_____	1
Stationary Lunge	Set 4: 6-8	_____	1
Step Ups	Set 5: 20	_____	0
Ball Squat			
Other_____			
CORE ABS			
Flat Crunch	_____		0.5
Twist Floor Crunch			
Incline Crunch			
Leg Raise			
Twisting Ball Crunch			
Ball Rollouts			
Other_____			
CHEST (P)			
Flat Bench Press	Set 1: 13-15	_____	1
Incline Bench Press	Set 2: 10-12	_____	1
Machine Press	Set 3: 8-10	_____	1
Dumbbell Fly	Set 4: 6-8	_____	1
Push Ups	Set 5: 20	_____	0
Dumbbell/Ball Press			
Dumbbell/Ball Fly			
Other_____			

Page 1

Workout 1

(Choose one)

Exercises	Reps	Lbs.	Rest (Min.)

CORE ABS

Flat Crunch	_____		0.5
Twist Floor Crunch			
Incline Crunch			
Leg Raise			
Twisting Ball Crunch			
Ball Rollouts			
Other_____			

SHOULDERS (S)

Dumbbell Press	Set 1: 13-15	_____	1
Machine Press	Set 2: 10-12	_____	1
Dumbbell Side Raise	Set 3: 8-10	_____	1
Dumbbell Rear Squeeze	Set 4: 6-8	_____	1
Dumbbell/Ball Press	Set 5: 20	_____	0
Band Side Raise			
Other_____			

CORE ABS

Flat Crunch	_____		0.5
Twist Floor Crunch			
Incline Crunch			
Leg Raise			
Twisting Ball Crunch			
Ball Rollouts			
Other_____			

TRICEPS- ARMS (S)

Tricep Pushdown	Set 1: 13-15	_____	1
French Curls	Set 2: 10-12	_____	1
Rope Pushdowns	Set 3: 8-10	_____	1
One Arm Pushdowns	Set 4: 6-8	_____	1
Chair Dips	Set 5: 20	_____	0
Dumbbell/Ball Kickbacks			
Other_____			

Page 2

231

Workout 2

Always: Warm-up with an eight- ten minute light cardiovascular exercise of choice, then start with a warm-up set using fifty percent of what you will be lifting on your first set and also stretch between sets. Fill in the chart below by selecting an exercise from each muscle group and filling in the pounds you lifted for each repetition.

(Choose one)

Exercises	Reps	Lbs.	Rest (Min.)
BACK OF THIGH (P)			
Laying Leg Curls	Set 1: 13-15	_____	1
Dumbbell Dead Lifts	Set 2: 10-12	_____	1
Reverse Lunge	Set 3: 8-10	_____	1
Stationary Lunge	Set 4: 6-8	_____	1
Ball Curls	Set 5: 20	_____	0
Dumbbell Leg Curls			
Other_____			
CORE ABS			
Flat Crunch	_____		0.5
Twist Floor Crunch			
Incline Crunch			
Leg Raise			
Twisting Ball Crunch			
Ball Rollouts			
Other_____			
CALVES (P)			
Standing Raise	Set 1: 13-15	_____	1
Seated Raise	Set 2: 10-12	_____	1
Leg Press	Set 3: 8-10	_____	1
One Leg Raise	Set 4: 6-8	_____	1
Two Leg Dumbbell Raise	Set 5: 20	_____	0
Other_____			

Page 1

Workout 2

(Choose one)

Exercises	Reps	Lbs.	Rest (Min.)
CORE ABS			
Flat Crunch	_____		0.5
Twist Floor Crunch			
Incline Crunch			
Leg Raise			
Twisting Ball Crunch			
Ball Rollouts			
Other_____			
BACK (P)			
Straight Bar Pull Down	Set 1: 13-15	_____	1
Close Grip Pull	Set 2: 10-12	_____	1
Seated Row	Set 3: 8-10	_____	1
Reverse Grip Pull Down	Set 4: 6-8	_____	1
Dumbbell Row	Set 5: 20	_____	0
Band/Desk Row			
Two Arm Dumbbell Row			
Other_____			
CORE ABS			
Flat Crunch	_____		0.5
Twist Floor Crunch			
Incline Crunch			
Leg Raise			
Twisting Ball Crunch			
Ball Rollouts			
Other_____			
BICEPS- ARMS (S)			
Dumbbell Curl	Set 1: 13-15	_____	1
Barbell Curls	Set 2: 10-12	_____	1
Barbell Preacher Curls	Set 3: 8-10	_____	1
Dumbbell Hammer Curl	Set 4: 6-8	_____	1
Dumbbell/Ball Seated Curl	Set 5: 20	_____	0
Dumbbell/Ball Preacher Curl			
Other_____			

Page 2

Cardio

Cardiovascular Exercise
Do your cardio three to five times a week.
(Choose one)
Bike; Bleachers; Elliptical; Sprints; Track; Treadmill; Other
Time / Duration:
MPH (speed):
Level:
Target Heart Rate:
 # Of Bleachers / Sprints:

Cardiovascular Exercise
Do your cardio three to five times a week.
(Choose one)
Bike; Bleachers; Elliptical; Sprints; Track; Treadmill; Other
Time / Duration:
MPH (speed):
Level:
Target Heart Rate:
 # Of Bleachers / Sprints:

Cardiovascular Exercise
Do your cardio three to five times a week.
(Choose one)
Bike; Bleachers; Elliptical; Sprints; Track; Treadmill; Other
Time / Duration:
MPH (speed):
Level:
Target Heart Rate:
 # Of Bleachers / Sprints:

Page 1

Cardio

Cardiovascular Exercise
Do your cardio three to five times a week.
(Choose one)
Bike; Bleachers; Elliptical; Sprints; Track; Treadmill; Other
Time / Duration:
MPH (speed):
Level:
Target Heart Rate:
 # Of Bleachers / Sprints:

Cardiovascular Exercise
Do your cardio three to five times a week.
(Choose one)
Bike; Bleachers; Elliptical; Sprints; Track; Treadmill; Other
Time / Duration:
MPH (speed):
Level:
Target Heart Rate:
 # Of Bleachers / Sprints:

Chapter Eleven

The Desert/Plateau & Your Insatiable Hunger

*...do not harden your hearts as you did in the rebellion, **during the time of testing in the desert...***

Hebrews 3:8

Remember, for everything in the spiritual there is a reflection found in the physical. Just as the physical desert is dry, hot and barren, so is the spiritual desert.

When a person truly goes looking for the Lord to surrender their hearts, they are certain to end up in the desert. When a person begins a health and fitness program, especially a weight loss one, they are also sure to end up in the desert...a desert *plateau*. The desert/plateau is that place where things are stagnant and nothing is changing. It is the final stop before entering into the "Promised Land", before going on to the work that the Lord has called you to. The desert/plateau is the place between you and the remaining weight you have yet to lose to achieve your final goal.

It's that part of the physical walk with God where there needs to be isolation. There can't be any distractions. The ambition of a career, the hope of a relationship, the preoccupation of a goal; nothing can distract you from your relationship and trust in God. The desert/plateau is the place of utter dependence and need. There is no water, no food, no shelter, and no security. The only comfort we can take is in knowing that just like for the Lord, Father has the angels attending to us too while we are there. (Mark 1:13)

Knowing that we are called to pick up our cross and follow Jesus, having similar experiences, it shouldn't be any surprise to us, whether physically healthy or not, when we end up in the desert. If you look at the greatest heroes of the bible, in both the Hebrew Testament and the New Testament, they all spent time in the desert. Moses, Caleb, Joshua and Paul are just a few of the greatest examples. God gave each of them promises through visions and afterward they ended up spending years in the desert training and being tested. And like these great men, if Father has a mark on your life and wants to use you greatly in the Kingdom, you can bet you too are going to spend some time in the desert. Do not be surprised at this. The desert was Jesus last stop prior to the start of His mission to save the world. *Then Jesus was led by the spirit into the desert to be tempted by the devil. After forty days and forty nights, he was hungry.* (Matthew 4:1-4)

Now let's look at the desert experience in detail. Notice that it says He was *led* by the Spirit; he was not forced to go. Its worth noting that people do not have to go to the desert nor do they have to stay there if they don't want to. Remember, we do have free will. However, if you opt out of the desert experience, it is certain that you will not receive all of your promised blessings and inheritance and it is likely that you will cause yourself unnecessary and painful experiences. (The story of Jonah is a great example of this.)

I have seen so many people start their physical walk with God only to quit after entering the desert. For some it feels too lonely, for others it feels too physically demanding, for others still they falsely believe they cannot control their hunger or desires and that God and His word are not enough to sustain them. These are all lies as we learned and previously discussed the truth in chapter nine.

We have to know and believe that it is God's will for us to be tested through sacrifice and that God's tests are designed and set up for us to pass. It is *satan* who tempts us and it is his temptations that set us up to fail God's tests.

Further along in the same story of Jesus time in the desert, we see that He was tempted while hungry during a 40 day fast. *"The tempter came to him and said, "If you are the son of God, tell these stones to become bread. Jesus answered "It is written: 'Man does not live on bread alone, but on every word that comes from the mouth of God.'*

Notice Jesus temptation only occurred <u>after</u> he was tired and hungry. During our times of fatigue and hunger is when we are the most vulnerable to sin and our enemy knows and uses this knowledge all too well. Dr. Charles Stanley, author of the book "Walking Wisely", advises that we should always remember the acronym H.A.L.T. so that we can remind ourselves to never become too **h**ungry, **a**ngry, **l**onely, or **t**ired. Using this principle will help us to remain less vulnerable.

Also, notice how Jesus counter attacked the lies of satan. He used the Word of God! Remember the word is our only weapon for fighting back. Not knowing the word of God is like going into a sword fight without a sword. You will lose!

Specifically addressing the issue of hunger, because that is one of the greatest obstacles in our quest for optimal physical health, we need to realize that hunger can sometimes be useful. I used to come from the physical school of thought that my clients should not skip meals but instead should eat on a regular basis. And for the most part I still feel the same way. But if a person finds themselves in the desert/plateau it is for a reason. Some obstacle, some desire, some stronghold has to be conquered. At this point in a person's physical walk with God I actually advocate fasting for both spiritual and physical reasons.

Jesus knew and taught that by the willful and sacrificial diminishment of our own human power and energy that we could gain God's attention and receive God's power and favor. In the Hebrew Testament we find examples of His power and favor gained through fasting by the great servant leaders and prophets including Moses, Elijah, Daniel, and Nehemiah.

We also know that in the New Testament Jesus told the disciples that prayer and fasting, was sometimes necessary. *When Jesus saw that a crowd was running to the scene, he rebuked the evil spirit. "You deaf and mute spirit," he said, "I command you, come out of him and never enter him again." The spirit shrieked, convulsed him violently and came out. The boy looked so much like a corpse that many said, "He's dead." But Jesus took him by the hand and lifted him to his feet, and he stood up. After Jesus had gone indoors, his disciples asked him privately, "Why couldn't we drive it out?" He replied, "This kind can come out only by prayer and fasting"* (Mark 9:25-29)

While we should never deliberately starve ourselves for weight loss; during a plateau, if done for spiritual and physical reasons fasting and prayer can be affective in helping us drive out unhealthy, unwanted body fat and the uncontrollable desires we have for the wrong kinds and wrong quantities of food.

Fasting literally means the act or practice of abstaining from or eating very little food. It is a period of abstention or self-denial especially used as a spiritual *discipline*. Fasting has been a practice in most religions and is without a doubt a spiritual purification rite. Both Christianity and Judaism encourage fasting for a variety of reasons. Those reasons include penitence, preparation for ceremony, purification, mourning, sacrifice, and the development of wisdom and power.

While all of those are spiritual reasons for fasting there are also great physical reasons to fast. Fasting can be used to treat or alleviate the symptoms of the following; colds and flu, constipation or diarrhea, insomnia, asthma, rashes, heart disease, diabetes, obesity, back pain, fatigue, allergies and fever.

Fasting is not limited to just the idea of food either. As indicated in Mark 9:25-29 prayer should often accompany fasting. There have been times during fasts when in order to pray more I have denied myself the luxuries of television and entertainment. Getting physically and spiritually healthy requires a deep commitment and great sacrifice.

For those of you who are questioning the validity of the idea of fasting altogether consider the natural instinct of animals. The first thing that animals do when they are sick or injured is find a safe place to rest near water so that they can drink and heal. Aren't we supposed to be more intelligent and more advanced than the animals? But what is the first thing we do when we're sick? Most of us take cold tylenols or some other over the counter medicine to treat our symptoms rather than starve out or detoxify the cause of our illness.

If you're questioning the validity of fasting you can also consider what God commanded in Leviticus 25:4: *But in the seventh year the land is to have a Sabbath of rest, a Sabbath to the Lord. Do not sow your fields or prune your vineyards.*

By following this law, this command, the Israelites were not practicing crop rotation, but instead the "fallow year", the year the crops were not planted. This essentially served the same purpose. It created a fast for the land and gave the land time to restore itself naturally. So if God designed the animals to heal from fasting and the land to regenerate itself from fasting don't you think fasting has application for you and me?

So having determined that fasting and the sacrificial denying of ones self is both spiritually and physically healthy, then how do we go about doing it in a safe way?

There are several types of fast. The first is the complete fast in which a person consumes neither any liquids nor foods. While some consider this the only true way of fasting, as a preventative health care professional I cannot advocate this method. I have *never* denied myself the necessary amount of water needed for the body during any of my personal fasts. I have however, abstained from all solid foods and consumed water only for up to 48 hours. To remain consistent with the food guidelines listed earlier in this book I always recommend drinking at least half of your body weight in ounces of water per day.

During a water only fast it is likely that you will suffer from extremely low amounts of energy which will make everyday normal functioning difficult. Even carrying on a simple conversation can become challenging. Fasts of this nature should only be done for spiritual reasons and should be done on weekends or during times when you are not responsible for work or the care of others. This type of fast is extreme and a person should always consult or be monitored by a physician if the fast is going to last longer than a day or two.

Another type of fast, and the one I actually recommend for my clients who find themselves in the desert/plateau, is the juice fast. While the water only fast has powerful spiritual and detoxification benefits, the juice only fast is more consistent with the bodies needs for *healthy weight loss*. Remember the body will not let go of unwanted fat stores if they are not replaced or if it is denied the nutrients it needs to function.

The juice fast is healthier because it still encourages detoxification and alkalization of the body but without the weakness from low energy associated with the other types of fasts. In addition, with a low and proper amount of nutrients and calories coming from fruits and vegetables it is more likely that the body will not metabolize (or eat up) its own muscles for energy. We didn't go into it earlier in the book because as I stated this book was not intended to be scientific, but muscles and muscular tone are important for energy and the metabolizing of fat. Without adequate calories, muscular atrophy which is commonly associated with complete and water only fasts, occurs and increases a person's possibility of losing the physical benefits of weight loss.

Please note that a juice only fast should consist of fresh squeezed fruits and vegetables and not store bought prepared juices. The store bought prepared juices have been processed in a way that causes them to lose vital nutrients including their live enzymes.

There are other types of fasts and fasting can be very complex but in keeping with the idea of this book I want to limit the amount of scientific information I expose you to. My recommendation to those of you who are on a physical walk with God and who are having trouble with a spiritual break through, or unanswered prayers, as well as those of you who are having trouble with physical break throughs such as additional weight loss after an initial period of success; is to try fasting.

To do this you will need a juicer. There are several different kinds available ranging in quality and price. I recommend starting with the simple Jack La Lannes' Power Juicer because of its price and reliability. Cheap juicers, typically anything under $70, maybe more trouble than they are worth. Be sure to do some shopping around to get the juicer that is right for you. All good juicers should also come with a recipe book.

In addition to purchasing a juicer, there are several notable books on the matter of fasting including "Fasting and Eating for Health" by Joel Fuhrman, "Fasting for Spiritual Break Through - A Guide to Nine Biblical Fasts" by Elmer L. Towns, and "Commonsense Guide to Fasting" by Kenneth E Hagin. I highly recommend reading a book specifically on fasting prior to undergoing one.

As a person fasts they will usually experience hunger that lasts for two or three days and then departs, at which point many people surprisingly feel a deep abdominal peace. Some people however, may continue to feel extremely hungry. If this is you, you should ask yourself what am I really hungry for? Fasting is an excellent time to work on your psychological connections to consumption and not just consumption of food.

I have found that when I am truly seeking God I am not hungry for anything other than his affection in my life. The sound of His voice is sweeter than anything I could ever eat. When I awake in the morning I am more eager to feed on His Word which fulfills my deep, intense spiritual hunger, before I ever even consider eating breakfast.

But if that is not you? Then what are you really hungry for? Is it food, money, to win, to find a spouse, maybe career advancement, sex or drugs?

Regardless of what your hunger is for, the pattern is always the same. We always find fulfillment in whatever it is we are consuming at the time, but it never lasts, it is never enough. It is always only a temporary fulfillment. If the fulfillment from those things was indeed lasting, we would not continually be in a search (hunger) from one experience to another and from vice to vice.

Having learned that, I propose that the truth is the only thing we should be and are really hungry for, is God. If you have an insatiable hunger for anything other than God then the following scripture is for you. *I will tend them in a good pasture, and the mountain heights of Israel will be their grazing land. There they will lie down in good grazing land, and there they will feed in rich pasture on the mountains of Israel. I myself will tend my sheep and have them lie down, declares the Sovereign Lord.* (Ezekiel 34:14-15)

God promises that He "Himself" will tend to us, feed us "good", and give us rest. So if this is the case why are so many of us trying to provide these things for ourselves?

Have you ever noticed that when you do get tired of something in your life, like food or alcohol and you are ready to move on to something new there is always a period of rest that comes in between before you pick up another vice or unhealthy habit. There is always that period of time where you gave something up, or lost it, and you are trying to figure out what is next. That is the time and place where the Lord is trying to tend to you. He tends you to lie down and rest so you can feed on the truth of His word, as opposed to the malnourishment you were receiving from whatever else you were feeding on.

Still not sure about this hunger being satisfied by the feeding of God? Here are two more scriptures...

Psalm 23:1-2

The Lord is my sheperd, I shall not be in want (hunger). He makes me lie down in green pastures, he leads me beside quiet waters, he restores my soul.

Isaiah 65:13

"My servants will eat, but you will go hungry; My servants will drink, but you will go thirsty.

How much more clearly can it be? Serve God alone, seek Him; and you will not be hungry.

But how do we know these scriptures are in fact parables and analogies for our spiritual feeding instead of just physical feeding for sheep? We know by the following statement from Jesus. *The disciples came to him and asked, "Why do you speak to the people in parables?" He replied, "The knowledge of the secrets of the kingdom of heaven has been given to you, but not to them. Whoever has will be given more, and he will have in abundance* (he will not hunger). *Whoever does not have, even what he has will be taken from him.* (he will hunger) *This is why I speak in parables: Though seeing, they do not see; though hearing, they do not hear or understand."* (Matthew 13:10-13)

The question is, do **you** see? Do **you** hear? Do **you** understand?

I want to finish out this section by going back to the movie the Field of Dreams. As I mentioned in the beginning of this chapter I have seen many people fall short of achieving great physical and spiritual health because they chose to opt out of their desert experience and could not break through their plateau. They did not go the distance. In the movie Field of Dreams the voice that kept calling to Ray was also telling him to "Go the Distance". I am telling you right now the same thing…Go the Distance!!

In what area of your life are you being called to go the distance? Have you lost a lot of weight and still have that last ten or twenty pounds to go? Are you at a point in your marriage where you're considering the alternatives to the covenant that you made before God? Are you in a business situation that is overwhelming and you have more than enough justifiable reasons to walk away and give up? Don't! Whatever going the distance means to you, it is important that you do it because in James 1:12 it says,

Blessed is the man who perseveres under trial, because when he has stood the test, he will receive the crown of life that God has promised to those who love Him.

How do you know that the trial or tribulation you are faced with is not being used to teach the people around you about Faith in God? Perhaps other people are learning about Faith by observing how you respond to your particular situation? Perhaps any *suffering* you are experiencing right now is for a far greater reason than you can imagine. Do not get caught up in the circumstances of your situation. Believing in God and following His biblical promises and truths does not mean that you will not have troubles in this world. However, it does mean that you will overcome them. It says in John 16:33, *in this world you will have trouble. But take heart! I have overcome the world.*

Stay focused on the biblical promises of God, remaining *patient* and *disciplined* in your circumstances, having the right *attitudes*, willing to *suffer* in your desert experience knowing that you were created in the healthy *self-image* of God and that with His *support* and His commitment to your *covenant,* that your *accountability* will be rewarded with the great spiritual and physical health we all desire. All at once the Spirit will lead you out just like He led you in. You will overcome...you will conquer. When it is all over and done with, your unhealthy hunger will be gone and you'll be like Timothy able to proudly say, *I have fought the good fight, I have finished the race, I have kept the Faith.*(2 Timothy 4:7)

Chapter/Week Eleven
Spiritual Workout

1. Why does the Holy Spirit lead us into desert experiences during our lifetime? What purposes do they serve?

_____

_____

_____

_____

_____

_____

_____

2. When was the last time you had a desert experience? Did you pass the test or did you choose to go back to the way things were before?

_____

_____

_____

_____

_____

_____

_____

_____

_____

3. What do you hunger for in your life? How can you starve that hunger in a healthy way?

_____

_____

_____

_____

_____

_____

_____

_____

_____

_____

4. What spiritual or physical break through is God calling you to?

_____

_____

_____

_____

_____

_____

_____

_____

5. What does James 1:12 say about the man or woman who goes the distance?

_____

_____

_____

_____

_____

_____

_____

_____

_____

Workout 1

Always: Warm-up with an eight- ten minute light cardiovascular exercise of choice, then start with a warm-up set using fifty percent of what you will be lifting on your first set and also stretch between sets. Fill in the chart below by selecting an exercise from each muscle group and filling in the pounds you lifted for each repetition.

(Choose one)

Exercises	Reps	Lbs.	Rest (Min.)
THIGHS (P)			
Leg Press	Set 1: 13-15	_____	1
Squats	Set 2: 10-12	_____	1
Leg Extensions	Set 3: 8-10	_____	1
Stationary Lunge	Set 4: 6-8	_____	1
Step Ups	Set 5: 20	_____	0
Ball Squat			
Other_____			
CORE ABS			
Flat Crunch		_____	0.5
Twist Floor Crunch			
Incline Crunch			
Leg Raise			
Twisting Ball Crunch			
Ball Rollouts			
Other_____			
CHEST (P)			
Flat Bench Press	Set 1: 13-15	_____	1
Incline Bench Press	Set 2: 10-12	_____	1
Machine Press	Set 3: 8-10	_____	1
Dumbbell Fly	Set 4: 6-8	_____	1
Push Ups	Set 5: 20	_____	0
Dumbbell/Ball Press			
Dumbbell/Ball Fly			
Other_____			

Page 1

251

Workout 1

(Choose one)

Exercises	Reps	Lbs.	Rest (Min.)
CORE ABS			
Flat Crunch	_____		0.5
Twist Floor Crunch			
Incline Crunch			
Leg Raise			
Twisting Ball Crunch			
Ball Rollouts			
Other_____			
SHOULDERS (S)			
Dumbbell Press	Set 1: 13-15	_____	1
Machine Press	Set 2: 10-12	_____	1
Dumbbell Side Raise	Set 3: 8-10	_____	1
Dumbbell Rear Squeeze	Set 4: 6-8	_____	1
Dumbbell/Ball Press	Set 5: 20	_____	0
Band Side Raise			
Other_____			
CORE ABS			
Flat Crunch	_____		0.5
Twist Floor Crunch			
Incline Crunch			
Leg Raise			
Twisting Ball Crunch			
Ball Rollouts			
Other_____			
TRICEPS- ARMS (S)			
Tricep Pushdown	Set 1: 13-15	_____	1
French Curls	Set 2: 10-12	_____	1
Rope Pushdowns	Set 3: 8-10	_____	1
One Arm Pushdowns	Set 4: 6-8	_____	1
Chair Dips	Set 5: 20	_____	0
Dumbbell/Ball Kickbacks			
Other_____			

Page 2

252

Workout 2

Always: Warm-up with an eight- ten minute light cardiovascular exercise of choice, then start with a warm-up set using fifty percent of what you will be lifting on your first set and also stretch between sets. Fill in the chart below by selecting an exercise from each muscle group and filling in the pounds you lifted for each repetition.

(Choose one)

Exercises	Reps	Lbs.	Rest (Min.)
BACK OF THIGH (P)			
Laying Leg Curls	Set 1: 13-15	_____	1
Dumbbell Dead Lifts	Set 2: 10-12	_____	1
Reverse Lunge	Set 3: 8-10	_____	1
Stationary Lunge	Set 4: 6-8	_____	1
Ball Curls	Set 5: 20	_____	0
Dumbbell Leg Curls			
Other_____			
CORE ABS			
Flat Crunch		_____	0.5
Twist Floor Crunch			
Incline Crunch			
Leg Raise			
Twisting Ball Crunch			
Ball Rollouts			
Other_____			
CALVES (P)			
Standing Raise	Set 1: 13-15	_____	1
Seated Raise	Set 2: 10-12	_____	1
Leg Press	Set 3: 8-10	_____	1
One Leg Raise	Set 4: 6-8	_____	1
Two Leg Dumbbell Raise	Set 5: 20	_____	0
Other_____			

Page 1

253

Workout 2

(Choose one)

Exercises	Reps	Lbs.	Rest (Min.)
CORE ABS			
Flat Crunch	_____		0.5
Twist Floor Crunch			
Incline Crunch			
Leg Raise			
Twisting Ball Crunch			
Ball Rollouts			
Other_____			
BACK (P)			
Straight Bar Pull Down	Set 1: 13-15	_____	1
Close Grip Pull	Set 2: 10-12	_____	1
Seated Row	Set 3: 8-10	_____	1
Reverse Grip Pull Down	Set 4: 6-8	_____	1
Dumbbell Row	Set 5: 20	_____	0
Band/Desk Row			
Two Arm Dumbbell Row			
Other_____			
CORE ABS			
Flat Crunch	_____		0.5
Twist Floor Crunch			
Incline Crunch			
Leg Raise			
Twisting Ball Crunch			
Ball Rollouts			
Other_____			
BICEPS- ARMS (S)			
Dumbbell Curl	Set 1: 13-15	_____	1
Barbell Curls	Set 2: 10-12	_____	1
Barbell Preacher Curls	Set 3: 8-10	_____	1
Dumbbell Hammer Curl	Set 4: 6-8	_____	1
Dumbbell/Ball Seated Curl	Set 5: 20	_____	0
Dumbbell/Ball Preacher Curl			
Other_____			

Page 2

254

Workout 1

Always: Warm-up with an eight- ten minute light cardiovascular exercise of choice, then start with a warm-up set using fifty percent of what you will be lifting on your first set and also stretch between sets. Fill in the chart below by selecting an exercise from each muscle group and filling in the pounds you lifted for each repetition.

(Choose one)

Exercises	Reps	Lbs.	Rest (Min.)
THIGHS (P)			
Leg Press	Set 1: 13-15	_____	1
Squats	Set 2: 10-12	_____	1
Leg Extensions	Set 3: 8-10	_____	1
Stationary Lunge	Set 4: 6-8	_____	1
Step Ups	Set 5: 20	_____	0
Ball Squat			
Other_____			
CORE ABS			
Flat Crunch		_____	0.5
Twist Floor Crunch			
Incline Crunch			
Leg Raise			
Twisting Ball Crunch			
Ball Rollouts			
Other_____			
CHEST (P)			
Flat Bench Press	Set 1: 13-15	_____	1
Incline Bench Press	Set 2: 10-12	_____	1
Machine Press	Set 3: 8-10	_____	1
Dumbbell Fly	Set 4: 6-8	_____	1
Push Ups	Set 5: 20	_____	0
Dumbbell/Ball Press			
Dumbbell/Ball Fly			
Other_____			

Page 1

255

Workout 1

(Choose one)

Exercises	Reps	Lbs.	Rest (Min.)
CORE ABS			
Flat Crunch	_____		0.5
Twist Floor Crunch			
Incline Crunch			
Leg Raise			
Twisting Ball Crunch			
Ball Rollouts			
Other_____			
SHOULDERS (S)			
Dumbbell Press	Set 1: 13-15	_____	1
Machine Press	Set 2: 10-12	_____	1
Dumbbell Side Raise	Set 3: 8-10	_____	1
Dumbbell Rear Squeeze	Set 4: 6-8	_____	1
Dumbbell/Ball Press	Set 5: 20	_____	0
Band Side Raise			
Other_____			
CORE ABS			
Flat Crunch	_____		0.5
Twist Floor Crunch			
Incline Crunch			
Leg Raise			
Twisting Ball Crunch			
Ball Rollouts			
Other_____			
TRICEPS- ARMS (S)			
Tricep Pushdown	Set 1: 13-15	_____	1
French Curls	Set 2: 10-12	_____	1
Rope Pushdowns	Set 3: 8-10	_____	1
One Arm Pushdowns	Set 4: 6-8	_____	1
Chair Dips	Set 5: 20	_____	0
Dumbbell/Ball Kickbacks			
Other_____			

Page 2

Cardio

Cardiovascular Exercise
Do your cardio three to five times a week.
(Choose one)
Bike; Bleachers; Elliptical; Sprints; Track; Treadmill; Other
Time / Duration:
MPH (speed):
Level:
Target Heart Rate:
 # Of Bleachers / Sprints:

Cardiovascular Exercise
Do your cardio three to five times a week.
(Choose one)
Bike; Bleachers; Elliptical; Sprints; Track; Treadmill; Other
Time / Duration:
MPH (speed):
Level:
Target Heart Rate:
 # Of Bleachers / Sprints:

Cardiovascular Exercise
Do your cardio three to five times a week.
(Choose one)
Bike; Bleachers; Elliptical; Sprints; Track; Treadmill; Other
Time / Duration:
MPH (speed):
Level:
Target Heart Rate:
 # Of Bleachers / Sprints:

Page 1

Cardio

Cardiovascular Exercise
Do your cardio three to five times a week.
(Choose one)
Bike; Bleachers; Elliptical; Sprints; Track; Treadmill; Other
Time / Duration:
MPH (speed):
Level:
Target Heart Rate:
 # Of Bleachers / Sprints:

Cardiovascular Exercise
Do your cardio three to five times a week.
(Choose one)
Bike; Bleachers; Elliptical; Sprints; Track; Treadmill; Other
Time / Duration:
MPH (speed):
Level:
Target Heart Rate:
 # Of Bleachers / Sprints:

Page 2

Chapter Twelve

The Ultimate Bodybuilders

"If one part suffers, every part suffers with it; if one part is honored, every part rejoices with it."

1 Corinthians 12:26

My fascination with weightlifting and body building began around age thirteen. Having been active and involved in athletics through all of my childhood it was only natural that my interest would expand to lifting weights in an effort to build my body up bigger and stronger.

At the time I started lifting weights the sport of bodybuilding was growing and becoming a mainstream staple. My initial introduction to it and my initial impression of it was shaped primarily by my exposure to muscle and fitness magazines. In the ensuing years my exposure to it was extended by television programming such as ESPN as well as various Hollywood movies and actors, all of which brought me to the surreal conclusion that the incredible physical achievements at the competitive level of bodybuilding were un-healthy and next to impossible without using harmful and illegal drugs.

Still, my passion for weightlifting never subsided. As the years progressed the sport in fact evolved and bodybuilding is no longer just some competitive sport found in dark sweaty auditoriums where drug using meatheads douse themselves in baby oil and flex their perfectly sculpted physiques.

No, today bodybuilding has been embraced by all walks of life. There is the CEO who has his trainer and realizes there is a connection between the discipline and passion of building his body and the discipline and passion of building his company. There is the stay at home mom who uses in home exercise videos and infomercial products to reshape her body after her pregnancy and to give her the strength and energy she needs to raise her children and take care of her home. There is also the casual athlete, the softball player, the cheerleader, or the runner that realizes bodybuilding training in the weight room can enhance their performances. All of these people are in their own right bodybuilders.

But what I want to make you aware of are *the ultimate bodybuilders.*

Now you are the body of Christ, and each one of you is a part of it. And in the church God has appointed first of all apostles, second prophets, third teachers, then workers of miracles, also those having gifts of healing, those able to help others, those with gifts of administration, and those speaking in different kinds of tongues (1Corinthians 12:27-28)

Even in the last chapter of this book the theme of my instructions to you still contend that for everything in the physical there is a spiritual reflection. Just as we have bodybuilders who build their physical bodies in the gym, we also have bodybuilders who build the spiritual body of Christ in the church.

We even have the analogy and proof given to us by Paul in the New Testament. *"The body is a unit, though it is made up of many parts; and though all its parts are many, they form one body. So it is with Christ. For we were all baptized by one Spirit into one body--whether Jews or Greeks, slave or free--and we were all given the one Spirit to drink. Now the body is not made up of one part but of many. If the foot should say, "Because I am not a hand, I do not belong to the body," it would not for that reason cease to be part of the body. And if the ear should say, "Because I am not an eye, I do not belong to the body," it would not for that reason cease to be part of the body. If the whole body were an eye, where would the sense of hearing be? If the whole body were an ear, where would the sense of smell be? But in fact God has arranged the parts in the body, every one of them, just as he wanted them to be. If they were all one part, where would the body be? As it is, there are many parts, but one body.* (1 Corinthians 12:12-20)

Yes, there are millions of people around the planet who are building the body of Christ and they are not all alike. They are each a unique part that serves a unique function. Some are pastors, some are nuns, some are not even apart of the clergy. There are the career professionals who are also building the body of Christ as well. For example, there are the physicians and nurses who use their gifts of healing on mission's trips to third world countries. There are the teachers who use their gifts to teach the children in Sunday school classes. There is the plumber who uses his gifts to fix the plumbing at his church at no charge because the church is struggling financially. And what about the business man who uses his talents and gifts to produce large amounts of wealth and then donates it for the causes of the Church? And then there is my personal favorite; how about the musician who rocks out during praise and worship leading us into the presence of God? Yes friends, bodybuilding is a glorious and grand sport to be participated in for the glory of God in faith believing we can all win the contest and that we can all build the biggest and most aesthetic body.

But what about you? What about your church? I have shown you that there is a physical walk with God that accompanies the spiritual one. But are you encouraging and participating in both walks or is it one over the other. I ask you to meditate on how anyone can effectively build the body on a spiritual level reaching the un-saved and the poor and needy if we are sick and un-healthy ourselves.

As if we didn't already know from our years in the church pews and from reading the bible that our physical health and caring for it is a mandate; but now we have books like this one specifically and further identifying the implication of it. Are we being honest with ourselves, our families, our church, and our congregations?

There is only one way for us to tell. In bodybuilding the mirror is the judge. It is the greatest tool for measuring results. The common belief among non-weightlifters is that mirrors are placed wall to wall in gymnasiums because of the vanity associated with the sport of bodybuilding but the truth is they are used as tools because it is the reflection in the mirror that showcases the truth; the results of the bodybuilder's efforts. It is the reflection which shows the results; the bigger bicep, the smaller waist, or the broader shoulders.

What do you see when you look in the mirror of your church? When you reflect on your church and its works what are the results? Is there greater attendance? Are there greater tithes and contributions? Is the church increasing its ability to give to the poor? In how many countries do you have a satellite church or how many ministries do you financially support around the world? Maybe the results of your church are great and can be seen around your community and or around the world. That's fantastic. If not, then maybe the concept or vision of "bodybuilding" is the answer you have been looking for.

Furthermore when it comes to bodybuilding we need to not only ask how many souls are being saved but how many souls are living and walking in victory? A saved soul that is continually tormented and living less than a life of victory wandering in the desert and not receiving the promises of God is a mockery of the message of Christ. Christ didn't stop at the cross. Yes, He died at the cross but He didn't stop there, he went beyond it! We need to get beyond it too and to do that we need to not just give birth to the body but continually build it.

What is the financial and physical shape of your church members? Do your members posses the land, owning their homes or are they still renting? Does every church member have a job? Are they involved in some kind of life team or ministry out reach or bible study outside of the regular worship services? These are all measures of how we are doing as bodybuilders. Are we building!!!??

When we look around the pews do our members look healthy or tired and out of shape? Are there people in your pews who are overweight or sick? Is there a proactive and aggressive preventative health care ministry in your church that receives not only appropriate training but also adequate fiscal attention? Is good physical health promoted and preached on from the pulpit but then left at that. It reminds me of the scripture I used earlier in this book.

Suppose a brother or sister is without clothes and daily food. If one of you says to him, "Go, I wish you well; keep warm and well fed," but does nothing about his physical needs, what good is it? (James 2:15-16)

What good is it for us to preach about the physical health of our members if we will not put our faith and finances in action to teach and promote it?

The Father is releasing a new anointing among men and women who are passionate *about the Physical walk with God.* The Father is imparting a word and knowledge to the church that as time marches on evil will further flourish and the fight will increase with intensity. The message is that the body needs to not only be strong in spirit but also strong in the flesh.

The body has the senior pastor who leads the church and with the apostolic vision. It has the associate pastors who over see the biblical counseling and restoration of the church members emotional health. It has the associate pastors who oversee the development of praise and worship, of children's and singles ministry, but *where is the pastor of health?*

Previously the YMCA and YWCA have carried the torch in a non-profit capacity encouraging greater physical health for the people in the community but with today's resources and the climate of today's economy it can be done on a much more effective manner at the church level.

All of these are tough questions to reflect on. Just as it is hard to be honest with yourself about the state of your individual health and as easy as it is to be in denial, it is just as hard for the church to look around at the neglected areas of the body of Christ and just as easy to also be in denial.

Now, with all of that said, how do we become the ultimate bodybuilders as is the name of this final chapter? To become ultimate bodybuilder both inside of the church and outside we have to be submitted to discipline and *authority*. It may seem like I am about to get side tracked here for a minute but keep reading and I will tie it all together.

We discussed discipline in chapter four so we won't get into that again but we do need to make and understand the connection between our submission to God's will and mandates and the authority or power that we carry in the earth.

Authority comes from submission to authority! That is the model Christ showed us. Submit to the Father, His will, and that is where your power will come from...that is where Jesus power came from....submission and obedience. Let me give you one more Hollywood example that illustrates the world's confused view point on authority to drive home my point.

Who's the Boss? aired for 8 seasons, premiering in September, 1984. The premise behind the show was that ex-baseball player, Tony Micelli (Tony Danza), wanted to move out of Brooklyn to find a better life for his daughter, Samantha (Alyssa Milano). As it turned out, ad-exec, Angela Bower (Judith Light), was in need of a housekeeper and a good male role-model for her son, Jonathan. Running into Tony at her apartment complex, Mona Robinson, Angela's mother, convinced Tony to apply for the job. After giving the matter careful thought, Angela decided to hire Tony. So began the show. Who's the Boss? captivated its audience, who wondered whether Tony and Angela would ever declare their unspoken love for each other and whether or not the question "Who's the Boss?" would ever be answered. Everyone wanted to know who the boss was...but they never found out!

So what is my point with this long synopsis of that sitcom? The point is this; unlike the mixed families on that show, you and I need to know who the boss is. The world can't continue being confused about who the boss is! Many of their family conflicts and the show's themes were a result of confusion or a lack of ordered authority *guided by biblical standards as opposed to the parent's or child's personal viewpoints.* As Christians we <u>must</u> claim our authority in the physical realms of our churches, work environments, and our homes. But in order to claim our established God given rightful inheritance of authority we have to first claim it in the spiritual realm.

Over the years I am sure many of you like me have been in situations where you were scratching your head and asking yourself...who's the boss? Why are my employees not listening to me? Why are my children not listening to me? If you're a professor or teacher you've probably wondered why your students weren't listening to you. Well, buckle your seatbelts for this one, maybe they are not the problem, maybe you are. You see, *everyone who is in a place of authority is also under authority*. This is one of the first biblical principles ever established by God Himself.

Genesis 2:15-17

The Lord God took the man and put him in the Garden of Eden to work it and take care of it. And the Lord God commanded the man, "You are free to eat from any tree in the garden; but you must not eat from the tree of the knowledge of good and evil, for when you eat of it you will surely die."

You see, at the same time God gave Adam authority to rule the garden *He also put Him under authority* with specific instructions. As we all know Adam failed to maintain obedience to the one rule God placed on him thus He lost the entire rule (authority) that He had over the garden. It wasn't until Jesus reacquired that authority through his utter and complete fulfillment of the law that man got it back. Once Jesus had submitted to all of God's rules and shed His innocent blood the authority was recaptured and later transferred to us by the Holy Spirit.

And why did God go to all of this trouble? We were given that authority for a reason. *I have given you authority to trample on snakes and scorpions and to overcome all the power of the enemy; nothing will harm you..."* (Luke 10:19)

We were given authority so that we could have authority over our sin because that is what connects us to Father and that is how He imparts miracles and blessings to the world through us.

When I look back over the course of my life I see the same rebellion in me that Adam exuded in the garden. This is absolutely embarrassing but of the nine jobs that I have had since age 15, I was either terminated or left four of them because of my rebellious nature toward the authority my bosses had over me. It didn't matter that some of them were insecure tyrannical egomaniacs who operated out of fear; all that mattered was that they were appointed as authority over me and I was rebellious. In my mind I thought I was rebelling against them. But since then, I have come to understand that I was actually rebelling against God in each of those situations. You see God placed them in authority over me. Paul teaches us *"Everyone must submit himself to the governing authorities, for there is no authority except that which God has established."* (Romans 13:1)

Authority is never self-appointed. After the last time I got fired I decided I would never work for anyone else ever again. I decided I would start my own business and that would take care of the problem I had with other people telling me what to do. (How wrong I was!) Even after I started my own business I still did not have authority. Wouldn't you know it; my employees wouldn't listen to me just like I wouldn't listen to my former bosses. How ironic is that? It was not until I submitted myself to the authority of God's rule in my life that things began to change. As I started setting the example of following a higher authority other than my own, things began to fall into place. Believe it or not people actually listen to me now.

So what about **your** authority? Are your experiencing the same problems I was having? Perhaps you should look to see if you are rebelling somewhere in your life. Maybe your kids overheard you talk trash to the police officer who wrote you a ticket and they are learning that rebellion directly from you. Or maybe the admin staff under you doesn't do what you tell them because they overheard you talking trash on the vice president who has authority over you. Or maybe your wife doesn't do some things you have asked her to do, because you're not submitted to God and the love that He requires you to lead with. Find the authority in your life, because there is one, and submit to it and it is likely that your situation will begin to change.

So why did I just go off on a tangent on authority when I was talking about building the body of Christ? It is because if we are going to be effective in the world, if we are going to be given the power to heal, the power to generate wealth, the power to lobby in government for laws that represent Christian morals and values; that authority has got to come from God and God can only give power to those individuals and groups that are submitted to His authority...His teachings, the teachings I have presented here.

So the questions still remain. Are you as an individual an ultimate bodybuilder? Is your church being effective as an ultimate bodybuilder in the community and world? Are you bodybuilding both spiritually **and physically**? If you're not or you're coming up short on your efforts then contact Healthy Images Preventative Health Care Organization today. That is why God commissioned our ministry. Let us get you or your church on *The Physical Walk with God*...walking in that place of obedience and with authority together as supportive parts in the ultimate body of Christ!

Chapter/Week Twelve
Spiritual Workout

1. Are you playing a role in the body of Christ? Are you helping to build it? How?

   _____

   _____

   _____

   _____

   _____

   _____

   _____

2. What area of your church do you think needs improvement? What will improve it and who do you need to meet with to get involved?

   _____

   _____

   _____

   _____

   _____

   _____

   _____

   _____

3. Who do you know either at home, work or church that needs to begin a physical walk with God and how are you going to introduce them to the idea of it?

   _____

   _____

   _____

   _____

_____

_____

_____

_____

_____

4. What spiritual principle must you follow to have authority and be able to be a blessing to the people and world around you?

_____

_____

_____

_____

_____

_____

_____

_____

_____

5. Review your lifestyle and list all of the areas where you have a rebellious attitude. Who can you submit to and or serve to show God you are serious about building the body of Christ?

_____

_____

_____

_____

_____

_____

_____

_____

_____

Workout 2

Always: Warm-up with an eight- ten minute light cardiovascular exercise of choice, then start with a warm-up set using fifty percent of what you will be lifting on your first set and also stretch between sets. Fill in the chart below by selecting an exercise from each muscle group and filling in the pounds you lifted for each repetition.

(Choose one)

Exercises	Reps	Lbs.	Rest (Min.)
BACK OF THIGH (P)			
Laying Leg Curls	Set 1: 13-15	_____	1
Dumbbell Dead Lifts	Set 2: 10-12	_____	1
Reverse Lunge	Set 3: 8-10	_____	1
Stationary Lunge	Set 4: 6-8	_____	1
Ball Curls	Set 5: 20	_____	0
Dumbbell Leg Curls			
Other_____			
CORE ABS			
Flat Crunch		_____	0.5
Twist Floor Crunch			
Incline Crunch			
Leg Raise			
Twisting Ball Crunch			
Ball Rollouts			
Other_____			
CALVES (P)			
Standing Raise	Set 1: 13-15	_____	1
Seated Raise	Set 2: 10-12	_____	1
Leg Press	Set 3: 8-10	_____	1
One Leg Raise	Set 4: 6-8	_____	1
Two Leg Dumbbell Raise	Set 5: 20	_____	0
Other_____			

Workout 2

(Choose one)

Exercises	Reps	Lbs.	Rest (Min.)

CORE ABS
Flat Crunch   _____   0.5
Twist Floor Crunch
Incline Crunch
Leg Raise
Twisting Ball Crunch
Ball Rollouts
Other_____

BACK (P)

Straight Bar Pull Down	Set 1: 13-15	_____	1
Close Grip Pull	Set 2: 10-12	_____	1
Seated Row	Set 3: 8-10	_____	1
Reverse Grip Pull Down	Set 4: 6-8	_____	1
Dumbbell Row	Set 5: 20	_____	0
Band/Desk Row			
Two Arm Dumbbell Row			
Other_____			

CORE ABS
Flat Crunch   _____   0.5
Twist Floor Crunch
Incline Crunch
Leg Raise
Twisting Ball Crunch
Ball Rollouts
Other_____

BICEPS- ARMS (S)

Dumbbell Curl	Set 1: 13-15	_____	1
Barbell Curls	Set 2: 10-12	_____	1
Barbell Preacher Curls	Set 3: 8-10	_____	1
Dumbbell Hammer Curl	Set 4: 6-8	_____	1
Dumbbell/Ball Seated Curl	Set 5: 20	_____	0
Dumbbell/Ball Preacher Curl			
Other_____			

Page 2

273

Workout 1

Always: Warm-up with an eight- ten minute light cardiovascular exercise of choice, then start with a warm-up set using fifty percent of what you will be lifting on your first set and also stretch between sets. Fill in the chart below by selecting an exercise from each muscle group and filling in the pounds you lifted for each repetition.

(Choose one)

Exercises	Reps	Lbs.	Rest (Min.)
THIGHS (P)			
Leg Press	Set 1: 13-15	_____	1
Squats	Set 2: 10-12	_____	1
Leg Extensions	Set 3: 8-10	_____	1
Stationary Lunge	Set 4: 6-8	_____	1
Step Ups	Set 5: 20	_____	0
Ball Squat			
Other_____			
CORE ABS			
Flat Crunch	_____		0.5
Twist Floor Crunch			
Incline Crunch			
Leg Raise			
Twisting Ball Crunch			
Ball Rollouts			
Other_____			
CHEST (P)			
Flat Bench Press	Set 1: 13-15	_____	1
Incline Bench Press	Set 2: 10-12	_____	1
Machine Press	Set 3: 8-10	_____	1
Dumbbell Fly	Set 4: 6-8	_____	1
Push Ups	Set 5: 20	_____	0
Dumbbell/Ball Press			
Dumbbell/Ball Fly			
Other_____			

Page 1

274

Workout 1

(Choose one)

Exercises	Reps	Lbs.	Rest (Min.)
CORE ABS			
Flat Crunch	———		0.5
Twist Floor Crunch			
Incline Crunch			
Leg Raise			
Twisting Ball Crunch			
Ball Rollouts			
Other_____			
SHOULDERS (S)			
Dumbbell Press	Set 1: 13-15	———	1
Machine Press	Set 2: 10-12	———	1
Dumbbell Side Raise	Set 3: 8-10	———	1
Dumbbell Rear Squeeze	Set 4: 6-8	———	1
Dumbbell/Ball Press	Set 5: 20	———	0
Band Side Raise			
Other_____			
CORE ABS			
Flat Crunch	———		0.5
Twist Floor Crunch			
Incline Crunch			
Leg Raise			
Twisting Ball Crunch			
Ball Rollouts			
Other_____			
TRICEPS- ARMS (S)			
Tricep Pushdown	Set 1: 13-15	———	1
French Curls	Set 2: 10-12	———	1
Rope Pushdowns	Set 3: 8-10	———	1
One Arm Pushdowns	Set 4: 6-8	———	1
Chair Dips	Set 5: 20	———	0
Dumbbell/Ball Kickbacks			
Other_____			

Page 2

Workout 2

Always: Warm-up with an eight- ten minute light cardiovascular exercise of choice, then start with a warm-up set using fifty percent of what you will be lifting on your first set and also stretch between sets. Fill in the chart below by selecting an exercise from each muscle group and filling in the pounds you lifted for each repetition.

(Choose one)

Exercises	Reps	Lbs.	Rest (Min.)
BACK OF THIGH (P)			
Laying Leg Curls	Set 1: 13-15	_____	1 .
Dumbbell Dead Lifts	Set 2: 10-12	_____	1
Reverse Lunge	Set 3: 8-10	_____	1
Stationary Lunge	Set 4: 6-8	_____	1
Ball Curls	Set 5: 20	_____	0
Dumbbell Leg Curls			
Other_____			
CORE ABS			
Flat Crunch		_____	0.5
Twist Floor Crunch			
Incline Crunch			
Leg Raise			
Twisting Ball Crunch			
Ball Rollouts			
Other_____			
CALVES (P)			
Standing Raise	Set 1: 13-15	_____	1
Seated Raise	Set 2: 10-12	_____	1
Leg Press	Set 3: 8-10	_____	1
One Leg Raise	Set 4: 6-8	_____	1
Two Leg Dumbbell Raise	Set 5: 20	_____	0
Other_____			

Page 1

276

Workout 2

(Choose one)

Exercises	Reps	Lbs.	Rest (Min.)
CORE ABS			
Flat Crunch	_____		0.5
Twist Floor Crunch			
Incline Crunch			
Leg Raise			
Twisting Ball Crunch			
Ball Rollouts			
Other_____			
BACK (P)			
Straight Bar Pull Down	Set 1: 13-15	_____	1
Close Grip Pull	Set 2: 10-12	_____	1
Seated Row	Set 3: 8-10	_____	1
Reverse Grip Pull Down	Set 4: 6-8	_____	1
Dumbbell Row	Set 5: 20	_____	0
Band/Desk Row			
Two Arm Dumbbell Row			
Other_____			
CORE ABS			
Flat Crunch	_____		0.5
Twist Floor Crunch			
Incline Crunch			
Leg Raise			
Twisting Ball Crunch			
Ball Rollouts			
Other_____			
BICEPS- ARMS (S)			
Dumbbell Curl	Set 1: 13-15	_____	1
Barbell Curls	Set 2: 10-12	_____	1
Barbell Preacher Curls	Set 3: 8-10	_____	1
Dumbbell Hammer Curl	Set 4: 6-8	_____	1
Dumbbell/Ball Seated Curl	Set 5: 20	_____	0
Dumbbell/Ball Preacher Curl			
Other_____			

Page 2

Cardio

Cardiovascular Exercise
Do your cardio three to five times a week.
(Choose one)
Bike; Bleachers; Elliptical; Sprints; Track; Treadmill; Other
Time / Duration:
MPH (speed):
Level:
Target Heart Rate:
 # Of Bleachers / Sprints:

Cardiovascular Exercise
Do your cardio three to five times a week.
(Choose one)
Bike; Bleachers; Elliptical; Sprints; Track; Treadmill; Other
Time / Duration:
MPH (speed):
Level:
Target Heart Rate:
 # Of Bleachers / Sprints:

Cardiovascular Exercise
Do your cardio three to five times a week.
(Choose one)
Bike; Bleachers; Elliptical; Sprints; Track; Treadmill; Other
Time / Duration:
MPH (speed):
Level:
Target Heart Rate:
 # Of Bleachers / Sprints:

Page 1

278

Cardio

Cardiovascular Exercise
Do your cardio three to five times a week.
(Choose one)
Bike; Bleachers; Elliptical; Sprints; Track; Treadmill; Other
Time / Duration:
MPH (speed):
Level:
Target Heart Rate:
 # Of Bleachers / Sprints:

Cardiovascular Exercise
Do your cardio three to five times a week.
(Choose one)
Bike; Bleachers; Elliptical; Sprints; Track; Treadmill; Other
Time / Duration:
MPH (speed):
Level:
Target Heart Rate:
 # Of Bleachers / Sprints:

Page 2

STOP!
You should consult a physician prior to starting any kind of exercise program.

IMPORTANT NOTE:
Do not do more than is instructed for any given day, or your results will vary. Before you start to workout, you need to review the exercise CD-ROM so that you have familiarized yourself with the exercises and correct form. You may also want to read the section on training tips.

Cardio:

Perform 25-50 minutes of cardiovascular exercise first thing in the morning (for optimal results). If you cannot do cardiovascular exercise in the morning, then do it anytime. Push yourself to where you can barely carry on a conversation for your entire duration time. You should do this three to five times per week but know that the more you do it the faster you will achieve the results you want. Remember the teachings on *discipline*.

Your cardio can consist of biking, walking or jogging, either indoors on a treadmill or outdoors; stair climbing, running bleachers, swimming or using an elliptical trainer.

Weight Training:

Warm-up: select one of the cardiovascular exercises listed, and warm-up for eight minutes, then stretch and begin weight training. This does not count as cardiovascular exercise time.

- Select your weight training exercises and cardiovascular exercises for the week ahead.

- Fill in your exercises; while working out, identify the number of reps completed during each set and fill in the amount of weight lifted for each set of each exercise using the exercise chart.

- Weight train three days per week consistently and intensely.

- Rest between sets for time instructed.

- Rotate Workout Plan 1and 2 each week for your first twelve weeks of training.

  EXAMPLE: Start week one with Workout Plan 1 then, day two do cardiovascular exercise, day three do Workout Plan 2, day four cardiovascular exercise, then day five back to Workout Plan 1 and day six cardiovascular exercise and rest on day seven. Alternate Workout Plans every other week. Start week two with Workout Plan 2, and repeat the cycle. Do Workout Plan 2, two times this week and Workout Plan 1 one time (do cardio on between days and/or at the end of each workout).

- Increase weight and your intensity level after each set (Refer to the Weight Increase Chart for weight increase estimations).

- All reps are the same in value, mix it up and do not get hung up always doing the same exercises or reps. You must do the repetitions that are suggested or your results will vary.

- If you miss a day, do the workout suggested, according to what day of the week it is.

Training Tips

I. Key Points to Remember while performing every Exercise.
   ☐ **S.T.A.R.T** - Always use these five key points while performing each weight training exercise.
      - **S** - Speed
      - **T** -Target Area
      - **A** -Alignment
      - **R** -Range of Motion
      - **T** -Tensions from both sides of the muscle
   ☐ Breath correctly, inhale on eccentric phase (negative), and exhale on concentric phase (positive)
   ☐ Slight pause with contraction
   ☐ No swinging or bouncing of movement
   ☐ Always be aware of posture
   ☐ Focus on negative phase as well
   ☐ Vary grips, stances, tempos, and ROM (range of motion)

II. Exercises
   1. Bench Press - pecs, anterior deltoids, triceps
      A. natural arch in back
      B. no lock out in elbows
      C. elbows parallel to floor
   2. DB Flys - pecs, anterior deltoids
      A. natural arch in back
      B. no lock out in elbows
      C. elbows parallel to floor
   3. Side Laterals - media and anterior deltoids, trapezious
      A. slight bend in elbow
      B. slight forward hip flexion
      C. natural curve in spine

4.   Shoulder Press - deltoids, trapezius, triceps
    A.   no lock in elbows
    B.   elbows parallel to floor
    C.   tight core, feet flat

5.   Tricep Extension (Pushdowns) - triceps
    A.   Soft bend in knees
    B.   natural curve in spine
    C.   slight retraction of scapula

6.   Skull Crushers (French curls) - triceps
    A.   feet flat on floor
    B.   humerous perpendicular to floor
    C.   tight core

7.   Leg Press - quads, hamstrings, glutes
    A.   no lock out in knees
    B.   postural alignment
    C.   no flexion beyond 90 degrees

8.   Squat - quads, hamstrings, glutes, AB, AD, lumbar, abdominals, entire core, back
    A.   no lock out on knees
    B.   postural alignment
    C.   no flexion beyond 90 degrees

9.   Leg Extensions - quads
    A.   no lock out in knees
    B.   no flexion beyond 90 degrees
    C.   no axis alignment

10.   Leg Curl - hamstrings, glutes
    A.   no lock out in knees
    B.   hips remain intact with bench
    C.   no swinging

11.   Lunges - quads, hamstrings, glutes, AB, AD, core
    A.   erect spine, tight core
    B.   knees over toes
    C.   femur parallel to floor (90 degrees)

12.   Lat Pull Downs - lats, traps, rhomboids, biceps, forearms
    A.   no lock out in elbows
    B.   keep chest high

C.   pull with scapula, not grip

13. <u>Bent Over Row</u> - rhomboids, lats, lumbar, biceps
   A.   soft bend in knees
   B.   natural curve in spine
   C.   torso parallel to floor

14. <u>Barbell Curl</u> - biceps, forearms
   A.   soft knees, tight core
   B.   slight hip flexion
   C.   no humeral movement

15. <u>Standing Calf</u> - soleous, gastrocnemius
   A.   soft bend in knees
   B.   firm ankle
   C.   natural cure in spine

16. <u>Crunch</u> - upper abdominals
   A.   lumbar remains flat
   B.   cradle neck, don't pull
   C.   limit ROM (range of motion)

17. <u>Opposite Arm and Leg</u> - lumbar, thoracic spine, glutes, hamstrings
   A.   slow contractions
   B.   hips remain intact with floor
   C.   unilateral or bilateral

Weight Increase Chart

IMPORTANT NOTE: This is only a suggestion to what kind of weight increase you can make according to the exercise list below. Only go up in weight if you reach the maximum number of reps suggested. Consult your physician before you start an exercise program.

Exercises	Female	Male
Legs		
Leg Press/Squat	10-30 lbs	20-60 lbs
Leg Curl / Leg extension	5-10 lbs	10-20 lbs
Calves	10-20 lbs	20-40 lbs
Chest		
Chest press	5-10 lbs	10-20 lbs
Chest flys	2 1/2 - 5 lbs	5-10 lbs
Back		
Lat pull downs	5-10 lbs	10-20 lbs
Rows	5-10 lbs	10-20 lbs
Shoulders		
Military Press	5-10 lbs	10-20 lbs
front / side raises	2 1/2 - 5 lbs	5-10 lbs
Arms		
Bicep curls	2 1/2 - 5 lbs	5-10 lbs
Tricep pushdowns	2 1/2 - 5 lbs	5-10 lbs

Definitions and Terms

PRIMARY MUSCLE GROUP (P)

- Chest
- Back
- Quads
- Hamstrings

SECONDARY MUSCLE GROUP (S)

- Shoulders
- Biceps
- Triceps
- Calves

(P) Primary muscles are the larger muscles that usually work in conjunction with the secondary muscles.

(S) Secondary muscles are the smaller muscles that sometimes help the larger muscles and can work without the assistance of the larger muscles.

Set - A group of repetitions followed by rest.

Repetition - The number of times an exercise is done during one set. (Refer to your CD-Rom for proper Range of Motion/Form)

"Sets and Repetitions"

Examples: **3x10-12 (P)** - do 3 sets of 10 or 12 repetitions for each **Primary** exercise chosen that day.

3x10-12 (S) - do 3 sets of 10 or 12 repetitions for each **Secondary** exercise chosen for that day.

How to Find a Good Trainer

Get a referral from a satisfied an already healthy looking friend or call nearby fitness centers, gyms or studios and find out what programs are offered by their personal trainers.

Find out if the trainer is certified by a nationally recognized body such as the American Council on Exercise (acefitness.org) or the American College of Sports Medicine (which requires a health-related academic degree). You should check to be sure dance or martial arts teachers have had proper training as well. These professional should also carry liability insurance. Check to be sure!

Schedule a trial workout to see if a trainer is suited to your personality and shows a genuine interest in you and your goals. This session should be FREE! If it isn't, find a trainer or gym who gives a session to "try before you buy."

Choose a personal trainer who has a good grasp on your workout level and who understands your physical limitations. Ask if they have experience in dealing with others with your same limitations. You want to work with someone who both motivates and challenges you but who doesn't set impossible goals or push you too fast or too hard.

Some gyms will only employ trainers who have a college degree in physiology or kinesiology. However, there are lots of graduates of weekend programs or, even worse, home-based or Internet classes. These people are not qualified to guide you in your health needs. Standardized fitness certification guidelines for the industry are pending; but in the meantime, check credentials *carefully*.

Check on your trainer's cancellation policy to avoid wasting money on appointments you can't make.

Expect to pay $40-$100 per individual sessions. If you find a trainer who works for less than $40 per hour it maybe a red flag that they are not qualified.

Many trainers will discount your hourly rate if you work out with a friend or in a group. You can find group training rates as low as $15-$20 per person based on the number of participants.

Remember that you can negotiate with trainers. If they don't meet your budget criteria, do not be discouraged, *you can still achieve great physical and spiritual health without one.*

ISBN 141208013-4